OVERLOOKED HERO:
A Portrait of Sir Sidney Smith

by

Joseph Hepburn Parsons
Edited and with Foreword by Tom Grundner

Fireship Press
www.FireshipPress.com

OVERLOOKED HERO: A Portrait of Sir Sidney Smith
Copyright © 2009 by Fireship Press

ISBN-13: 978-1-934757-62-8
ISBN-10: 1-934757-62-4

BISAC Subject Headings:
    BIO008000   BIOGRAPHY & AUTOBIOGRAPHY / Military
    HIS027150   HISTORY / Military / Naval
    HIS015000   HISTORY / Europe / Great Britain

This work is based on:
Parsons, J. H. (1914). *Historical Papers Upon Men and Events of Rare Interest in the Napoleonic Epoch* (Vol. 1). New York: Saalfield Publishing Co. pp. 131-237.

Address all correspondence to:
Fireship Press
P.O. Box 68412
Tucson, AZ 85737

Or visit our website at:
www.FireshipPress.com

1.0

OVERLOOKED HERO:
A Portrait of Sir Sidney Smith

To the Memory of my Father

The Late Honorable Lewis E. Parsons,
Governor of the State of Alabama,
A Profound Student of History,

WHOSE teachings first encouraged me in its
study, by revealing the true relationship
of many notable historical events in the
destinies of nations as well as of individuals,

THIS WORK
is gratefully and affectionately dedicated
by
The Author

Contents

FOREWORD
The Overlooked Hero

...to this hour it remains a mystery with me, why and how it came about, that in every distribution of honors Sir Sidney Smith was overlooked.

Thomas De Quincey
Author of *Confessions of an English Opium-Eater*

My introduction to Sir Sidney Smith began innocently enough.

I was starting work on a series of novels about a time-traveler by the name of Lucas Walker. He was to be a modern U.S. naval officer who is transported to various periods in time to undergo a variety of nautical adventures. His first exploit was to take place at the Battle of the Chesapeake (Battle of the Capes for you British readers), which sealed the fate of Cornwallis at Yorktown.

With my lead character (I thought) firmly in place, I needed to create some on-going co-stars. I wanted a female involved so I created the wise-cracking Susan Whitney. I needed a male foil for Walker and came across an historical figure who was actually at the Battle of the Capes. He was a young 17-year-old lieutenant named Sidney Smith.

Then a funny thing happened. Sidney Smith took over both the book and the series.

The more I learned about him, the more fascinated I became. His enormously complex personality, his bravery, and his flashes of sheer genius intrigued me. However, something was missing. Something just didn't add up.

In the nearly 170 years since his death there had been five biographies written about Sir Sidney. One came out in 1839 about a year before his death, another a few years later (1848), then three more in recent times (1964, 1975, and 1996). All were well written; all were interesting; and all were accurate—or at least as accurate as one can be when the subject is someone who lived 200 years ago.

I read them all, but the question that was at the heart of my confusion remained unanswered. Why was this man not hailed as the greatest British naval hero of all time? (Yes, even greater than Horatio Nelson!)

I had never heard of Sidney Smith; but I thought maybe that was because I am an American and not as attuned to the British pantheon of heros. Then I found out that not many British knew much about him either. Given his astonishing accomplishments, that amazed me; but I had recently become involved in a start-up publishing company and had little time for thinking about old Sir Sidney.

In September 2008, however, my schedule finally cleared enough to start work on the third of my Sir Sidney Smith novels. In my research, I came upon a lengthy chapter in a book written almost 100 years ago called: *Historical Papers Upon Men and Rare Events in the Napoleonic Epoch* by Joseph Parsons. Given that inviting title, it quickly found its way to my "read this some day... maybe" stack; but read it, I eventually did. And when I did—it electrified me.

The grand hero of the naval side of the Napoleonic Wars was Horatio Nelson. I knew that. Sidney Smith was a rival of Nelson. I knew that. He was a brilliant, but personally eccentric, naval officer; and he didn't suffer fools gladly. I knew those things as well.

But Parsons put the pieces together on some other things that I had never really thought about. In so doing, he makes the case that the single greatest hero of the Napoleonic Wars was not Nelson—it was Smith—and frankly, I have to agree.

Consider just three of his exploits. (And yes, there are more I could cite.)

* * *

In 1793, after war with France broke out again, Smith bought a ship with his own money and sailed from Smyrna, Turkey to Toulon where the British fleet was located. As the British were beating a hasty retreat, Smith volunteered to burn the French ships that had been trapped and captured in Toulon Harbor. In one night he destroyed 14 French ships—10 of them ships of the line—a single loss greater than anything the French had ever previously suffered. In addition, he destroyed numerous supply depots on shore. Nevertheless, Nelson complained because Smith had not done more.

In 1798, Nelson became famous when his 13 ships defeated 13 French ships at the Battle of the Nile, thus trapping Napoleon in Egypt. Now, suppose Smith had not traveled to Toulon on his own dime and hazarded himself to destroy those ships. Suppose, instead, the French had those 10 ships of the line that Smith burned (not to mention the warehouses), making it 13 British ships against 23 well-supplied French vessels. How might the Battle of the Nile have turned out? Would it have been fought at all; or might Nelson, the hunter, have become Nelson, the hunted?

* * *

In 1799, Napoleon marched north out of Egypt with 13,000 troops. His goal was to conquer Constantinople. With that accomplished, he could amass a staggeringly large (and rich) French/Ottoman army and either press east into India, or drive west through the back door of Europe, or eventually both. To get to Constantinople, however, along the way he had to capture the City of Acre. Literally days before Napoleon's appearance, Smith arrived with two British ships of the line and some smaller vessels, rebuilt the city's fortifications, and captured Napoleon's siege artillery. After a bloody two-month battle, Sir Sidney Smith, a naval officer, became the first person to defeat Napoleon head-to-head *on land*.

[iii]

While this was going on, Smith's superiors, Horatio Nelson and Admiral John Jervis, sat on their hands and did absolutely nothing to help. Later Nelson became immortal with his victory over the combined French and Spanish fleets at Trafalgar. What is rather clear, however, is that there would have *been* no Trafalgar if Smith had not defeated Napoleon at Acre.

* * *

In 1807, Spain and France had divided Portugal between them and Napoleon wanted very badly to capture Lisbon and the Portuguese royal family. The reason wasn't because he wanted the family so much as he wanted their treasury. The royal coffers contained an estimated 500,000,000 francs, and Napoleon desperately needed that money. Sir Sidney arrived on the scene and forced an indecisive royal family (and their treasury) to flee out of one end of town, literally as the French were entering the other.

If Napoleon had secured that wealth, would there have been an ill-fated Russian campaign in 1812? Would there have been an exile to Elba in 1814? Would there have been a Waterloo in 1815? Or, with the addition of that money, would the war have been long over by then?

* * *

In return for their services, Horatio Nelson became a Viscount and an immortal national hero. Field Marshall Arthur Wellesley, of Waterloo fame, became a Duke. Admiral John Jervis, who was miles away from the battle in which he won his peerage, became an Earl. And Sir Sidney?

In 1799, Sir Sidney Smith received a £1000 a year allowance, which, most of the time, the government forgot to pay.

In 1815, he was made a Knight Commander in the Order of the Bath, the second-highest rank, in the order. He is finally a British Knight; but it is a distinction usually awarded to officers "for good, but ordinary services."

In 1838, when Smith was 74 years old, Queen Victoria promoted him to Knight Grand Cross of the Order of the

Bath. Thus, while lesser men were routinely being elevated to peerages, and after a lifetime of unbelievable service, he was awarded the highest rank—in the fourth-highest order of knighthood. It would be the top award he would ever receive from his government, as he died two years later.

I am sorry; but if it is possible for Queen Elizabeth to bestow a peerage posthumously, I think she should do just that.

When Napoleon wrote in his memoirs: "That man made me miss my destiny," he was not referring to the Duke of Wellington. He was not referring to Horatio Nelson. He was referring—very specifically—to Sir Sidney Smith.

This book is a terrific portrait of that man.

As a final note, I edited this manuscript primarily to change it from Parson's rather ponderous Victorian writing style to something a bit more amenable to the modern reader. I don't think I substantively altered anything that he said, or was trying to say; but if errors have been introduced, I apologize. The fault is mine and not Mr. Parsons.

Tom Grundner
Tucson, Arizona

CHAPTER ONE
ADMIRAL OF THE RED

Before getting to the stories, let me introduce you to the man—Sir William Sidney Smith or, as he is better known, Sir Sidney. I want to introduce you to him as others, both friends as well as foes, saw him in the years when he was at the very height of his career. With that in mind, we can then follow his marvelous life, although what follows will hardly be a complete introduction.

We are told that:

He was, in many essentials, utterly unlike those who achieved for England her proudest naval victories. He would have dared more, and probably have done more—yet, we think, have risked too much. After all, so much in a naval combat depends upon accident, that success more often attends upon too much, than upon too little, risk. Still, had Sir Sidney attained any great naval command, there was danger of his not being able to resist the fascinations of the splendid, the magnificent, and the chivalrous, both in treaty and in fight, to the neglect of the stern, the hard, and the usefully successful. Even in his limited commands, refined notions of honour have saved the enemy from destructive broadsides that could have been poured in at an advantage, and which few, besides himself, would have deemed unfair. [1]

As far as his personal appearance goes:

> He had an air of general smartness and was extremely gentlemanly in his deportment. He had a good humored, agreeable manner with him, with a certain dash and turn of chivalry that was very taking with the ladies... He was, generally, very showily dressed, perhaps with some singularity; but there was not a particle of coxcombry about him. [2]

A French officer of high rank, who met him during the campaigns in Egypt and Syria, described his impressions as follows:

> Though small in stature, he had all the appearances that indicate a brave and generous-hearted man with a fine dark countenance, and eyes which sparkled with intelligence. His very appearance showed that he possessed an ardent imagination, which naturally prompted him to form and execute bold and important enterprises; he seemed, as it were, *to be born to deserve glory and to acquire it.* [3]

Coming from an enemy, that is no small testimonial to the dignity of his presence.

Yet, views on Sir Sidney were deeply divided. It was also said that:

> ...such are his qualities, that his friends are very friends indeed, and verge too much upon idolaters; and his enemies are condemning sceptics of anything good or great about him. Whilst the one party would

---

[1] Howard, E. (2008). *The Memoirs of Sir Sidney Smith*. Tucson, AZ: Fireship Press. p. 369.

[2] Ibid., p. 178.

[3] Ibid., p. 135.

extol him, as the *ne plus ultra* of heroism, the other would designate him merely as a successful charl-atan—brave, but without conduct, cunning without being sensible—arrogant and supercilious in his youth, and, in his after life, immersed in the vapours of his intolerable vanity; that all that ever was sterling in the man is totally evaporated, and that nothing remains of him but a gaudy shell, tricked out with ribbons and stars, and all the blazonry of which beggarly monarchs are so lavish, and fools so greedy. [1]

In what follows I hope to demonstrate that this last description, while a common one, is in no way accurate. He was, in truth, a great commander who was actively denied the full opportunity to prove it.

* * *

William Sidney Smith was born June 21, 1764, in Park Lane, Westminster, and was the second son of Captain John Smith of the Guards. His father, being a gentleman usher to Queen Charlotte, had the influence to secure his appointment as a midshipman when he was only twelve years of age, and place him on board the ship-of-the-line *Sandwich* (90-guns) under Lord Rodney. [2]　However improper this sort of favoritism might appear today, in the Royal Navy of Smith's time it was not at all unusual. Great admirals such as Duncan, Lord Jervis, and even Lord Nelson himself, all entered the service at about the same age and by the same means.

In 1780, when he was 16, Admiral Rodney appointed him a lieutenant on the *Alcide* (74). Although he had passed his

---

[1] Ibid., p. 191.

[2] *Editor's Note* – Smith actually entered the navy at age 11 as a "captain's servant" and was later promoted to midshipman. He served first aboard the *Tortoise*, a 32 gun armed storeship, then aboard the frigate *Unicorn* (28), a few months aboard the *Arrogant* (74), and *then* (at age 15) served on the *Sandwich* (90) under the famous Admiral George Brydges Rodney. The author is quite right, though; his method of entrance into the navy was not at all unusual at that time.

lieutenant's examination, his promotion was not officially confirmed until August 29, 1783 because there was an Admiralty rule saying you had to be at least 19 years old to hold that rank. He served in the British fleets on the coasts of America, and was present in the action between Admiral Graves and the French fleet off Chesapeake Bay [Battle of the Capes]. He was also at Admiral Rodney's great victory over the French in the West Indies on April 1, 1782 [Battle of the Saints].

On the second of May 1782, he was made commander and was appointed to the *Fury* (16), having served as a lieutenant for less than a year. In 1783, he made post-captain, when he was only nineteen—an irregularly rapid promotion that might be attributable to a combination of merit and his father's influence with Queen Charlotte. Nevertheless, it turned out to be fully justified by his subsequent career.

In this manner, two years before he attained his majority as a citizen, as a naval officer he ranked with a full colonel in the British army. He obtained with this promotion the *Alcmene* frigate of 32 guns. However, peace had been declared between Great Britain, France, and the United States, and he was soon ordered back to England where his ship was paid off.

The youthful captain quickly fell into the swirl of London society; but he also took advantage of this period to travel—first to France to perfect his language skills (and to spy on French seaports), then to Spain and Morocco. In 1790, he took advantage of the rupture between Sweden and Russia, and entered the naval service of the former, while many of his fellow-officers entered service with Russia. They were all adventurers—soldiers of fortune—and seeking the excitement of active service.

Sidney Smith participated in many of the bloody naval engagements that followed between the Swedish and Russian fleets. It was, in many ways, a sad spectacle as the courage and skill of these English officers were as effectively employed in the slaughter of each other as against the Swedes and Russians. As a result, many of the English officers on both sides were grievously wounded or perished. The Captains Trevenor and Dawson were among the slain, and Captain Marshall, having been mortally wounded, refused to surrender his ship, which sunk with him and his crew, with its colors still flying in melancholy glory and defiance.

At the great naval battle of Svensksund, in the Gulf of Finland and not very far from St. Petersburg, the Russian fleet met defeat. They sustained a loss of 11,000 killed, drowned, or captured, together with the capture or destruction of most of their ships. Though the King of Sweden was nominally in command, Captain Sidney Smith stood at the King's side during the entire engagement, lasting twenty-four hours, encouraging the latter when the tide of battle set against them, and directing the battle through the King.

During the action, an English officer by the name of Denison commanded the Russian frigate *Venus*, and nearly captured the King of Sweden. Sidney Smith, observing the seaman-like way in which the *Venus* bore down on the royal galley, turned to the King and said, "Your majesty, that ship must be commanded by an Englishman!" [1] It was a hint that they needed to depart.

Knowing their small galley could not contend against a large frigate, they fled to another and safer vessel in a small boat that was lying alongside. While the *Venus* eventually took the royal galley, they missed the objective of their daring action. The attack was soon avenged, however, for under the orders of the King and Smith, an overwhelming force of Swedish ships quickly enveloped the *Venus*, destroying her after Captain Denison and most of her crew had perished in a most heroic defense.

---

[1] Ibid., p. 18.

This great victory was, after some time had elapsed, followed by the Peace of Reichenbach. Upon the conclusion of peace, the Swedish naval service no longer appealed to Smith, who accordingly resigned his commission. He was decorated with the Swedish Grand Cross of the Order of the Sword by the grateful monarch who would gladly have retained him in his service. On May 16th, 1792, his own sovereign, George III, was pleased to confirm his Swedish knighthood.

As Great Britain continued at peace, service at home held no attraction for the restless spirit of Sir Sidney. Being sated with fashionable society in England, he took service in the Turkish navy, hoping for a chance for more fighting and further distinction.

Here we find him in 1793, when war broke out again between Great Britain and France. He immediately resigned from the Turkish service; and, finding about forty English seamen out of work at Smyrna, he hired them all, purchased a swift lateen-rigged craft, and sailed down the Mediterranean in search of the English fleet. He found them at Toulon.

He arrived a short time before the English and their Spanish and Neapolitan allies were driven out of Toulon by the genius of the youthful Napoleon. Thus, for the first time, Napoleon and Smith encountered each other and began a struggle that would become forever memorable.

CHAPTER TWO
THE DESTRUCTION OF TOULON

Toulon, the great naval port on the Mediterranean was, with the connivance of the French royalists, surrendered to the English and their allies. It contained a large fleet of French warships, moored in the docks but without crews, and vast quantities of naval stores of all kinds. French units, under a young, unknown, officer named Bonaparte, succeeded in capturing the key forts that overlooked Toulon Harbor. This forced the allies to pull out of the harbor in great haste. The original idea was to carry away as many French ships as possible, and to burn the rest along with the storehouses. This, however, was now not possible.

Such was the terror and confusion in the crowded port of Toulon, that the allied commanders had abandoned any attempt at executing that plan. Overwhelmed with the task of getting their motley army of 12,000 British, Spanish and Neapolitan troops with its artillery embarked, and burdened with almost 15,000 terrified royalist civilian inhabitants, they were worried that any further delay might endanger their own fleet.

By this time Sir Sidney Smith had reported in to Lord Hood, the commander-in-chief, on board his flagship *Vic-*

tory, and he at once volunteered to burn the French fleet and arsenals. It was a feat that was deemed impracticable with the small means that could then be spared for the purpose. Nevertheless, with a few small gun-boats, and a mixed force of English and Spaniards, Smith destroyed fourteen of the French ships—ten ships of the line, two frigates, and two corvettes—together with the immense mast house, several of the great store houses and other buildings.

In some ways, however, that was a mixed blessing. The burning warehouses, filled with rosin, tar, turpentine, and other inflammable material, shed a prodigious light over the whole harbor, city, and surrounding country. That light enabled the French batteries to begin bombarding every part of the city and port, adding fresh horrors to an already terrible scene. In the midst of this, the Spaniards blew up two large ships loaded with immense quantities of powder—ships which Sir Sidney had specifically ordered to be scuttled and sunk, not burned. This resulted in explosions so tremendous that they produced the effects of an earthquake—destroying much property, and breaking every window glass in the harbor vicinity. In the confusion, Sir Sidney beat off several attacks, and despite enemy efforts to destroy his boats, reached the allied fleet with fewer losses of men than might have been expected.

The sad remnants of those civilian royalists, who had neglected to go off in the first embarkation, now rushed to the beach and begged the aid of their British friends. Mothers clasping their babes to their bosoms, children, decrepit old men, rushed in terror to the water's edge, and Sir Sidney instantly suspended his retreat and began rescuing as many people as he could. Unfortunately, nearly half the French fleet escaped destruction because some of his Spanish allies could not, or would not, obey his orders. [1]

---

[1] *Editor's Note* — It turned out later that the Spanish admiral, Don Langara, had been bribed to undermine and hinder the British evacuation of Toulon.

As a reward for this magnificent act of heroism and service to his country, Lord Hood made him the bearer of the dispatches to England, containing an account of the events leading to the abandonment of Toulon. Included was a report of Smith's splendid actions, which, in fact, were the only actions that reflected glory on anyone connected with that ill-conducted expedition. He received an enthusiastic welcome, and was treated with distinction at the Court and at the Admiralty. However, he received no other rewards, nor promotion, though he had just struck a blow at the French naval power that was second only to Trafalgar in the loss of ships, and far greater than that in the loss of material and supplies. [1]

Mention was, in fact, made of his great services at Toulon from the throne. But, as Sir Sidney himself afterwards said: "...your memorialist, being then a half-pay officer, acting as a volunteer, though under the admiral's authority and orders, I was not considered as entitled to any share in the distribution of the gratuity to the fleet, nor did I receive any other recompense whatever for that service." [2]

It is not too much to say that the blow, delivered by Sir Sidney at Toulon, so weakened French naval power that it completely changed the whole course of events between England and France in the Mediterranean, in Egypt, and the East.

Consider for a moment the following.

---

[1] *Editor's Note* – Admiral Hood had sent Horatio Nelson to Sardinia and Naples with dispatches, so he was nowhere near the disaster at Toulon. Yet, with regard to Smith's actions, Nelson wrote: "Sir Sidney Smith did not burn them all. Lord Hood mistook the man: There is an old song, 'Great talkers do the least, we see.'" Nelson's close friend, Cuthbert Collingwood, wrote similar sentiments, although Collingwood was comfortably cruising around the English Channel and, like Nelson, was nowhere near Toulon. It was the first shot in a life-long enmity between Nelson and his followers, and Smith.

[2] Barrow, J. (2009). *The Life And Correspondence of Admiral Sir William Sidney Smith.* Tucson, AZ: Fireship Press. P. 79.

Suppose the thirteen poorly equipped ships of Admiral Brueys at the Battle of the Nile had been increased by, say, ten out of the fourteen ships destroyed by Sir Sidney at Toulon. Even more importantly, suppose the French had had access to the vast naval stores which Smith also destroyed, and could have put their entire Mediterranean fleet into first-class condition. If either of those things had occurred, in all likelihood, Lord Nelson would never have won the Battle of the Nile—if there would have been a battle at all.

If Brueys had had twenty-three well-equipped battle ships and encountered Nelson's fleet of only thirteen, the latter would almost certainly have been destroyed. Indeed, with that number of ships, Admiral Brueys probably would not have even *been* at Aboukir Bay. After landing Napoleon and his troops, he would have been out seeking the British, not the other way around. Given the lopsided advantage Brueys would have had, if he had found Nelson, he would probably have quickly disposed of him.

If that had occurred, one can only imagine what would have happened with an over-powering French fleet in supreme control of the Mediterranean. Reinforcements and supplies would have been available in any amount for Bonaparte's army in Egypt and Syria. With those supplies and reinforcements, and with the French dominating the sea-lanes, literally nothing could have prevented Bonaparte from occupying Constantinople and overthrowing the Ottoman Empire. With that city as a base of operations, and with the whole region as a vast recruiting ground, Bonaparte would have likely undermined the British efforts in India, and probably returned in triumph to Paris via Vienna and Munich. [1]

It is often said that Sir Sidney Smith made Napoleon "miss his destiny" by his heroic and successful defense of St. Jean d'Acre. [2] But, in truth, Smith began that process much earlier at Toulon by destroying the very means that would, to all appearance, have assured his conquest of the East.

A commander so able and daring as Sir Sidney was not to be kept in idleness. He was placed in command of the frigate *Diamond* (38) early in 1794; and was employed in blockade duty along the French coast, where he performed many daring actions and made numerous captures from the enemy.

The British government received information that the large French squadron at Brest had sailed, and was cruising on the open sea. They wanted Smith to verify that report. Sir Sidney decided to do this by taking his ship far enough into the bay to ascertain what shipping lay there.

In short order, he had the *Diamond* so "frenchified" in appearance that it completely deceived even the French. With the utmost coolness, he sailed past the forts into the harbor, stayed there all night, and departed early in the

---

[1] *Editor's Note* – Or, to put it in Napoleon's own words: "Yes, if I had taken Acre, I would have assumed the turban, I would have put the army in loose breeches; I would no longer have exposed it, except at the last extremity; I would have made it my sacred battalion, my immortals. It is with Arabs, Greeks, and Armenians that I would have ended the war against the Turks. Instead of one battle in Moravia I would have gained a battle of Issus; I would have made myself emperor of the East, and returned to Paris by the way of Constantinople." (Taine, p. 35)

[2] *Editor's Note* – Actually, the person who often said it, was Napoleon, e.g. "Had I but captured Acre, I would have reached Constantinople and the Indies; I would have changed the face of the world. But that man [Smith] made me miss my destiny." (Fitchett, p. 72)

morning, actually stopping to chat with a French ship-of-the-line on the way out! [1]

About this time, Sir Sidney was promoted to the rank of commodore. After a number of bold actions against the enemy to whom he had become a veritable terror, he fell in with and captured a large French lugger off the mouth of the Seine at Le Havre. After a furious battle, the captured ship and Smith's boarding crew were carried by the tide far up the river. As a result, he was captured the next morning before they could make their way back out to their ship again.

This act, so daring and offering no real gain relative to the risk involved, excited French suspicion that he was a spy; and he was confined in the Temple prison at Paris for two years. [2]

---

[1] *Editor's Note* — For an excellent fictional account of this adventure, as well as of the destruction of Toulon, see: Grundner, T. (2007). *HMS Diamond*. Tucson, AZ: Fireship Press.

[2] *Editor's Note* — It should be pointed out that the French were both right and wrong in their assessment of Sir Sidney as a spy. At the time of his capture, he might have been on an intelligence mission, but he was *not* spying. He was in full uniform and therefore could not be classified as a spy. However, from his prison cell in the Temple, he operated Britain's primary spy ring—the *Agence de Paris*—in one of the most outrageously daring (and least known) chapters of the war.

CHAPTER THREE
PRISONER

Efforts for his exchange were immediately made by the English government, but without success. The French were, by this time, fully acquainted with his actions at Toulon, Brest and elsewhere, and boasted of having in their hands the boldest and most active commodore in the British navy. The pressure against his exchange was evidently immense, as will appear by the following letter to General Edward Smith, Sir Sidney's uncle, from Mr. Dundas and forwarded by the former to Sir Sidney:

Walmer Castle, Tuesday morning.

Mr. Dundas presents his compliments to General Smith, and returns to him the last correspondence from Sir Sidney, which he has perused. Mr. Dundas is sorry to observe that the *arrêté* of the Directory there alluded to, by which Sir Sidney is susceptible of exchange, stipulates that this exchange shall be granted in return for four thousand French seamen—a condition so evidently inadmissible that Mr. Dundas cannot entertain an expectation that the prospect of Sir Sidney's return to England is thereby improved. [1]

Was the demand of the French Directory a mockery, or did they seriously considered it to be a fair exchange for our officer? If it's the latter, could they have paid him a greater compliment?

The hardships of Smith's imprisonment, however, we're not great. Indeed, it might be said not to have extended much beyond the loss of his liberty by being detained in Paris. The warden of the Temple prison, M. Lasne, [2] a generous-hearted man, soon conceived a great regard, as well as admiration for this bold English commodore. He regarded him not merely as a man of the highest courage but of the highest honor, and often had Smith dine with him in his own private quarters in the prison.

Sir Sidney writes that:

> One day when I dined with him, he perceived that I fixed my attention on a window then partly open which looked upon the street. I saw his uneasiness and it amused me; however, to put an end to it, I said to him, laughing, 'I know what you are thinking of but fear not. It is now 3 o'clock. I will make truce with you till midnight; and, I give you my word of honor that till that time, even were the doors open, I would not escape. When that hour is passed, my promise is at an end, and we are enemies again.' 'Sir,' replied he, 'your word is a safer bond than my bars and bolts; till midnight, therefore, I am perfectly easy.' When we arose from the table, the keeper took me aside, and speaking with warmth said, 'Commodore, the Boule-

---

[1] Howard, p. 402.

[2] *Editor's Note* — Smith's jailor at the time of this incident was Mutius Lasne. By the time of his escape, however, Lasne had been replaced by Antoine Boniface who received all the blame for Smith's rather abrupt departure.

vard is not far. If you are inclined to take the air there, I will conduct you.'

My astonishment was extreme, but I accepted the offer, and in the evening we went out. From that time forward this confidence always continued. Whenever I was desirous to enjoy liberty, I offered him a suspension of arms till a certain hour. This my generous enemy never refused; but when the armistice was at an end, his vigilance was unbounded... This man had a very accurate idea of the obligations of honor. He often said to me, "Were you even under sentence of death, I would permit you to go out on your parole, because I should be certain of your return." [1]

Smith spoke French like a native and, during these pleasant rambles about Paris, he managed to make some very agreeable acquaintances, including several charming ladies. Indeed, there was so much mutual confidence displayed that the captive and the keeper sometimes changed roles, the prisoner taking charge of the jailer. It seems the latter excellent soul would, now and then, indulge in so many *bons coups de vin* that not only care, but even assistance, was necessary to convey him back to the Temple. More than once, Sir Sidney actually had trouble being admitted back into the prison with his tipsy friend and companion.

However, these truces with the governor, once ended, did not prevent Sir Sidney from devising some means of escape. After several failures, his escape was secured by means of a stolen blank sheet of letterhead that had been signed by the Minister of Marine just prior to his departure on a trip. On this blank was set a skillfully forged order transferring him from the Temple prison to another prison in the city. These orders, of course, bore the genuine seal of the Ministry of

---

[1] *Editor's Note* — It's hard to know which account Parsons is citing here. I have six different printings of this story with publication dates ranging from 1799 to 1841. The earliest being: "Account of Sir Sidney Smith's Imprisonment and Escape." *The British Critic*, Vol. XVI, July-December, 1799, pg. 540.

Marine, secured by devoted friends in Paris. Through their aid, also, he made his way to the coast and eventually to England. By a strange sort of coincidence, Sir Sidney arrived home on the 8th of May 1798, just ten days before Bonaparte's fleet began leaving for Egypt. [1]

Within a few months it was apparent that the invasion of Egypt by the French would lead to difficulties with Turkey, which claimed sovereignty over that country. The British government was naturally eager to encourage this feeling by inducing the Turks to conclude an alliance with Great Britain. To accomplish this, it was decided to bestow diplomatic status upon the English officer who would be sent to obtain that alliance.

That officer was Sir Sidney.

---

[1] *Editor's Note* — As another coincidence, the Minister of Marine, from whom the blank document was stolen, was Georges René Le Peley de Pléville, M. de Pléville achieved initial fame as a young man for saving the life of a British officer by the name of John Jervis when his ship foundered off the coast of Provence. As Lord St. Vincent, that same John Jervis would later in life become a profound enemy of Sidney Smith.

CHAPTER FOUR
INDEPENDENT COMMAND IN THE
MEDITERRANEAN

The man best fitted for such a mission—who had just escaped from a French prison, and had served in the Turkish naval service for a short time—presented himself, as he had at Toulon, at the precise moment of need for his services.

Among several aspirants for the honor of such a command the choice fortunately fell upon the most capable of them all, Sir Sidney Smith; and he was named as joint-plenipotentiary with the British ambassador at Constantinople, who was his brother, Mr. Spencer Smith.

Sir Sidney was appointed to command a fine ship-of-the-line, the *Tigre*, of 84 guns, which was equipped with unusual care, bountifully supplied with the finest stores of provisions and fully manned with a picked crew of able seamen. Shortly thereafter, they sailed for the eastern Mediterranean upon one of the most memorable, as well as honorable, missions of his career.

His instructions were to proceed to Constantinople to negotiate an alliance between Great Britain and Turkey against France for their unprovoked invasion of Egypt.

Success in this task was not difficult as the Turks were already so incensed over the French invasion that they immediately accepted all of the English proposals. They also had no trouble accepting the subsidies Britain offered to assist them in putting their fleets and armies upon a war footing.

Sir Sidney also bore several valuable presents from his Britannic majesty, George III, to the Grand Seignior, as a small token of the high regard entertained by the former for the latter. Among these gifts were twelve handsome brass field-pieces, engraved with the royal motto, "*Honi soit qui mal y pense*," [Evil be to him who evil thinks] with caissons so constructed as to be portable on camels.

That exalted ruler, treating the royal British present in the desired spirit, immediately sent them to the Ottoman armies to use for the slaughter of the French invaders. Unfortunately, it was afterwards learned that most of those fine cannons were, "by one of the inscrutable decrees of Allah, allowed to be taken from the faithful followers of the Only True Prophet, and used by the Infidel French dogs in the slaughter of the Grand Seignior's own brave troops and servants."

CHAPTER FIVE
MAKING ENEMIES: EARL ST. VINCENT
AND HORATIO NELSON

At this time, the first evidence of a jealous hostility to Sir Sidney, in high quarters, were openly shown. The reasons for this are many.

First, Sidney Smith was not fitted, either by habit or temperament, to act as second in command to anyone. [1]

Second, his highly prized appointment to, and continuance in, a separate command in the Eastern Mediterranean, was offensive to a lot of people in high places. This was especially true of the Earl St. Vincent [Admiral John Jervis], commander-in-chief of the British naval forces in that sea, and to his protégé, Rear-Admiral Horatio Nelson. It was so great an annoyance to Nelson that, after his own victory at the Nile, St. Vincent feared Lord Nelson would quit the royal Navy.

He wrote to Lord Spencer from Gibraltar that:

---

[1] *Editor's Note* — To put it in more contemporary terms, Sir Sidney simply did not suffer fools gladly—and there were no shortage of fools in the Royal Navy of that period. This characteristic of his would get him into trouble time and time again throughout his career.

An arrogant letter, written by Sir Sidney Smith to Sir William Hamilton when he joined the blockade off Malta, has wounded Rear-Admiral Nelson to the quick (as per enclosed) which compels me to put this strange man immediately under his lordship's orders, as the King may be deprived of his (Lord Nelson's) valuable services—as superior to Sir Sidney Smith at all times, as he is to ordinary men. I experienced a trait of the presumptuous character of this young man during his short stay at Gibraltar, which I passed over, that it might not appear that I was governed by prejudice in my conduct towards him. [1]

Historians would love to have access to these two letters, the one written by Sidney Smith and the reply by Nelson; but, alas, they are lost. Nevertheless, we know that Sir Sidney had little awe of Lord Nelson, and even less for the contemptible British ambassador at Naples, Sir William Hamilton. It might be imagined that Sir Sidney's letter referred to, in no flattering terms, Sir William's connivance at the open intrigue between his wife, the notorious Lady Hamilton, and Nelson. This ready willingness to confront powerful people often operated against Smith, and despite his brilliant services, was probably the main cause of his failure ever to be given a great naval command, for which he was undoubtedly fully qualified.

Once the treaty of alliance with the Sultan was concluded, Sir Sidney proceeded to draw up plans for a combined British-Turkish operation by land and sea against the French in Egypt. He proposed the assembly of 20,000 Turkish troops on the Island of Rhodes, whence they would be transported by sea for a descent upon the coasts of Egypt near Alexandria. Meanwhile, a second Turkish army of 50,000 men was to cross the desert from Syria and march upon Cairo. Both armies would be supported by all the

---

[1] Howard. p. 73.

Mamelukes and Arabs that Murad Bey could assemble in Egypt itself.

Bonaparte soon learned of Sir Sidney's plans. In response, he decided to open the campaign himself by marching against the Ottoman army then collecting in Syria, instead of waiting for the storm to burst upon his head in Egypt. For this purpose, he assembled all the troops that could be spared from the defense of that country, amounting, however, only to 13,000 men, including 900 cavalry and 49 field-pieces.

Sir Sidney being apprised of this intended movement, left Constantinople in the *Tigre* on February 19, 1799, and arrived off Alexandria on March 3. Once there, he joined the blockading squadron in vigorously bombarded its defenses. It was hoped that by doing so it would divert and delay Bonaparte long enough to allow the Turks to complete their preparations.

However, this bombardment of Alexandria produced no effect at all upon Bonaparte. He easily saw its intent, and pressed his march across the desert to Palestine. Seeing the failure of his efforts to delay Bonaparte's invasion, Sir Sidney, reinforced from the blockading squadron by the *Theseus* of 74 guns, and several small gunboats, then sailed in all haste for Acre. He arrived on the 15th of March, and the French army appeared there the next day. Recognizing the importance of Acre as the key to Syria and the East, and seeing the weakness of its defenses, Smith immediately landed his seamen and marines to both aid—and compel— the Turks to strengthen them in the few precious hours remaining before the French could attack.

The force of only two battleships that were allowed Sir Sidney for the defense of Acre, against such an army, led by a hitherto invincible conqueror, was ridiculously inadequate. During the desperate evenly balanced battle that raged without ceasing for sixty days, neither Lord Nelson nor the Earl of St. Vincent ever even attempted to reinforce him.

When he wasn't blockading Malta, Nelson was basking in the charms of the infamous Lady Hamilton, with whose "shawl dances", and *poses plastique,* he had become madly infatuated; and Admiral Jervis was lying idly at Gibraltar. Between the two of them, they had thirty or more ships; yet, somehow, not one could be spared for Sir Sidney's relief, or for the defeat of France's premier general.

The addition of even two more ships would have placed the result at Acre beyond doubt. Yet, it would seem his superiors, by their indifference to the interests of England as well as to the fate of Sir Sidney, had no other purpose or wish in view than to see him defeated and discredited. As a result, they simply left him to fight it out as best he could. In addition, as a possible alternate outcome, the chances of Smith being killed are always exceedingly good at such a place as Acre! [1]

Not even after his triumphant defense of Acre and the retreat of Bonaparte to Egypt, was Smith sufficiently strengthened to properly blockade Alexandria and patrol the coast. When Bonaparte eventually escaped back to France, Smith's only two major blockading ships were off-station. One, the *Theseus,* was absent undergoing repairs of damages

---

[1] *Editor's Note* — It could be argued that this willful withholding of support amounted, in effect, to an attempt to legally murder Sir Sidney. That might sound like an extreme conclusion, but consider the following. France's leading general was Napoleon. Smith had Napoleon pinned down at Acre. After their defeat at the Nile, the French fleet was no longer a significant factor. So, what could possibly have been taking place in the *western* Mediterranean that could be of a higher priority than (possibly literally) taking out Napoleon? Blockading Malta? And even if there were "other priorities," two months is enough time to send for ships and troops all the way from England, if need be. Yet, the ships and troops were withheld; and Sir Sidney was hung out to dry. I agree with the author that Nelson and Jervis fully expected Smith to fail; and if Smith were killed in the process, I am sure it would have been "most regrettable." Moreover, I think Smith knew what was going on. It is little wonder to me that, years later, Sir Sidney was among the few notables who did *not* attend Nelson's funeral, even though he was in London at the time and could have easily done so.

sustained from an explosion of shells (mentioned below), while the *Tigre* had gone to Cyprus for a fresh supply of water. If Smith had even had *one* other ship to leave on guard before Alexandria, the two small frigates of Bonaparte could never have emerged from that harbor, and thus would have obliged him to remain in Egypt during the crisis in France

What might the results of the war have been if Napoleon had not escaped back to France?

CHAPTER SIX
THE DEFENSE OF ACRE

At this time the Pasha of Acre was a ferocious, avaricious old Turk, Ahmed al-Jazzar, surnamed "the Butcher" [Djezzar] from the numerous cruel massacres he had inflicted on his enemies. Via merciless taxation extending over many years, he had accumulated a large treasure. He lived in magnificent splendor in his palace, in the midst of a large garden, with his numerous harems, which he tended to recruit by forcibly seizing and carrying off the prettiest Christian and Jewish maidens to be found in Syria.

The successive storming and capture of Gaza and Jaffa by the rapidly approaching French army had not shaken his belief in the defenses of Acre. He believed that, under the blessing and protection of Allah (to which he felt himself fully entitled) the city was impregnable to the Infidels. With his treasures, arms and artillery, he had shut himself up in that stronghold, determined to make the most desperate resistance with the aid of a garrison of about 6,000 well-armed and equipped janissaries and Albanians.

Acre, noted for its long sieges and the heroic exploits of Crusaders and Saracens around its walls, is situated on a peninsula, which enables the defenders to focus all their defensive efforts on the isthmus that connects it with the mainland. A single wall, with curtains flanked by square towers, and a wet ditch, constituted its sole means of defense; but in the right hands, it could be formidable.

The presence of the British squadron at anchor in the Bay of Acre served notice to the French general that the task before him would be a difficult one. The guns of the British squadron protected its entire waterfront, and could rake assaulting columns in flank. Sir Sidney and the Pasha used the small interval of time they had left in strengthening the defenses of the place in every possible manner.

The French took position before the walls, along a curving ridge of moderate elevation, not far distant. The following day, British picket-ships noticed several vessels coming around the headlands of Mount Carmel, not far from where the ancient brook of Kishon, of biblical fame, falls into the Bay of Acre. They were Napoleon's flotilla dispatched from Alexandria with the heavy guns, stores and platforms for the siege of the town. The French looked on helplessly as Sir Sidney captured them. These guns, 44 in number, were immediately mounted on the ramparts of Acre, and contributed greatly, in fact decisively, to the defense of the city.

At the same time there appeared at Acre, Colonel Phélippeaux, a French Emigrant officer of engineers, who offered his services to the Pasha, and exerted his talents, which were of a high order, in repairing and arming the fortifications. [1] In addition, Sir Sidney himself landed at the head of a large body of seamen and marines to aid in the

---

[1] *Editor's Note* — Picard de Phélippeaux came with Sir Sidney aboard the *Tigre*. A trained military engineer, he had a lifelong hatred of Napoleon that extended back to childhood when they literally sat on the same bench together as classmates at the *École Militaire*. Indeed, Phélippeaux was one of the people who arranged and participated in Sidney Smith's dramatic escape from the Temple Prison in 1798. Phélippeaux died at Acre, reportedly of exhaustion (sunstroke).

defense of the town. The capture of their siege guns was a great loss to the besiegers. It reduced their battering train to one 32-pound carronade, four 12-pounders, eight howitzers, and thirty 4-pound field guns.

Yet, such was the energy of the French engineers that when the Turks made a sortie on the 26th of March to stop their trenching, they were driven back into Acre with heavy loss. The French then dug a mine shaft under one of the principal towers, which was severely battered, despite a tremendous defensive fire from all the guns of the fortress, aided by the guns of the British ships in the Bay. Two days later, the mine was exploded and a practicable breach was created in the wall. The French grenadiers instantly advanced to the assault and running rapidly forward to the edge of the counterscarp were stopped by a ditch fifteen feet deep, which was only half filled up with rubble from the wall.

Their ardor speedily overcame this obstacle, however, and jumping into the ditch, they mounted on each other's shoulders and, under a murderous fire, climbed the opposite side securing a toehold in the ruined tower. The impediment of the counterscarp, however, prevented them from being adequately supported.

Turks in vast numbers were thrown against them and, after a desperate struggle, succeeded in expelling them from that part of the wall and driving them, with great slaughter, back into their own lines. At the same time, the Turks decapitated, according to their custom, all the dead and wounded French who could not be carried off by their comrades. These gory heads were brought in triumph to lay at the feet of the ferocious Djezzar in his palace, who bestowed liberal rewards upon those who brought in these ghastly trophies.

A second assault on the 1st of April met with no better success, and the French troops were withdrawn back into their works to await the arrival of several heavy guns, sent from Egypt by sea to Jaffa and thence by land to Acre. Both sides labored incessantly to strengthen their positions, and the heavy artillery of the besieged kept up an incessant fire upon the besiegers who had no adequate means of responding.

Meanwhile the Turks were collecting their forces on the other side of the River Jordan to raise the siege. The Mussulman populations of all the surrounding provinces had been aroused. The Mamelukes of Ibrahim Bey, who had escaped from Egypt, joined with the levies and the Janizaries of Hamah and of Homs, of Aleppo and of Damascus. These, in turn, joined with an immense horde of irregular cavalry from the Syrian Desert, and formed a vast army, which the people of the country boasted was as "innumerable as the sands of the sea or the stars of heaven." They crossed the Jordan by the Bridge of Jacob to attack the French troops posted around Canna in Galilee and Nazareth—names and scenes forever memorable in Christian annals.

Sir Sidney and Djezzar Pasha knew that Bonaparte would not wait for this Mussulman army to attack him in his entrenchments before Acre, where he would thus be between two fires. They knew that he would have to divide his forces in order to march to encounter the Pasha of Damascus who was advancing through the mountains of Naplouse. So, the two men decided to attack the French as soon as they were weakened by Napoleon's departure.

On the 9th of April, a grand sortie of Janizaries, headed by the English officers, and supported by marines from the fleet, took place and obtained some success at first. But, by an uncommon exertion of vigor in the French lines, the sortie was finally repulsed with dreadful slaughter, including Major Oldfield of the British royal marines, who fell in one of the trenches of the French lines.

A furious struggle ensued for the possession of his body. The British marines tried to drag it away by his neck-cloth, whereupon a mighty French grenadier drove a pike clear through it into the earth and thus held it so firmly that the neck-cloth gave way. The remnants of the marines were obliged to leave the body of their commander with the enemy who, it must be said, buried it with fitting military honors.

Another burial service, illustrative of the conditions between the English and French, occurred soon after this. It is given, as authentic, in Edward Howard's interesting memoirs of Sir Sidney Smith, and, somewhat abridged, is as follows:

A heavy, stupid sort of ordinary seaman from the *Tigre*, while serving his turn on the shore in the trenches, had noticed the body of a French general, splendid in his uniform, lying exposed in the very centre of the narrow space between the opposing trenches, and it dwelt upon his mind to such an extent that he determined, at all risks, to give to this glittering dead enemy a decent burial, and not suffer him to rot among the heaps of dead French and Turks, lying thickly around, and poisoning the air with an almost unbearable stench, but which neither side would grant a truce to bury.

Nothing divided the hostile entrenchments but this narrow sort of street, and so closely placed were the foes to one another that even a low conversational tone could be heard from one embankment to the other, above which nothing appeared but a line of bayonets, for if a hat or a head, or any object, appeared on either side it was instantly saluted with a volley of bullets.

It was about noon, and the respective hostile lines were preserving a dead silence, anxiously watching for the opportunity of a shot at each other. Our seaman, without having mentioned his purpose to any one, had provided himself with a spade and a pick-axe, and suddenly broke the ominous silence by shouting out, in a stentorian voice: "Mounseers, a-a-hoy!!! 'Vast heaving there a bit will ye? And belay over all with your poppers for a spell!!" And then shoved his broad, ruddy, unmeaning countenance over the lines. Two hundred muskets instantly covered him, but seeing him with only his peaceful implements, and not exactly understanding his demand for a parley, the French forbore to fire, while Jack very leisurely scrambled over the entrenchment into the open space, paying no further attention whatever to the hostile muskets, but, going to the dead French general, he took his measure, and proceeded to dig a grave alongside him. When this was finished, shaking what was so lately a French general, very cordially and affectionately by the hand, he reverently placed him in his grave, shoveled the earth upon, and made all smooth above him.

When he had finished, he made his best sailor's bow and foot-scrape to the Frenchmen looking on, shouldered his implements, and climbed back into his own quarters with the imperturbability that had marked his appearance, amidst the hearty cheers of both sides. Jack only remarked that now he should sleep better with this off his mind.

A few days later, another French general, in his resplendent uniform, came aboard the *Tigre* on some matter of negotiation, after completing which he expressed an anxious desire to see the interrer of his late comrade and friend. Jack was summoned, and praised for his heroism in an eloquent speech of which he hardly understood a word, though it was interpreted to him. The general then offered him a purse filled with gold pieces, which he was at first unwilling to accept, but finally satisfied his scruples by telling the general that "he would be glad to do the same thing for him, as he had done for his friend—for nothing!" A courtesy which the gallant general smilingly begged to be excused from undergoing, and said *au revoir* to all. [1]

The struggle between the besieged and the besiegers grew daily in intensity, with heavy losses to both sides. The season was advancing; March with its chilly winds had gone, and April gave way to May and its lengthening days for mutual slaughter. The short warm spring nights were bathed in a great golden moon, and further lit up by the gleam of thousands of bright stars in the Syrian skies. The breezes were as soft as those of Italy, but the curse of the mosquito was upon the land with the coming of May, almost banishing sleep. The mosquitoes got so bad that the troops on both sides, who had no means of protection against such a pest, saw the return of the day with all its horrors and dangers as almost a welcome relief.

The thunder of over three hundred guns, afloat and ashore, reverberated in the east. They were heard beyond the Jordan, the Waters of Merom and the Sea of Galilee. They were heard with awe far to the south amid the hills of Judea, where peaceful shepherds wandered with their flocks. They were heard away into the west, across the blue waves of the Mediterranean. However, the sound of that ceaseless roar of cannons upon Acre's desert strand, telling of brave men dying in heaps, fell upon deaf ears at Naples and Gibraltar. During those two months not only ships, but English troops—from England itself even—might have been sent by Lord Nelson or the Earl of St. Vincent. Such a move would have preserved Acre from all danger of capture, and aided its heroic defender, whose energy and courage only rose higher as he realized what this cold desertion and betrayal meant.

The bloody defeat of the grand sortie of April 9th with the full strength of the garrison and fleet by only half the French troops left to guard their lines, convinced Sir Sidney and Djezzar that Acre must have relief from without. Their principal hopes rested upon the great army of Abdallah,

---

[1] Howard. p. 99.

Pasha of Damascus, already advancing from the east to raise the siege.

Bonaparte had marched to the valley of the Jordan with a force scarcely six thousand strong—so far inferior, indeed, to the coming Turkish host of over 20,000 men, that his defeat seemed assured. After their arrival, the capture or destruction of the remainder of the French army would follow the combined attack of the garrison of Acre and the army of Abdallah Pasha.

They did not have long to wait for news of the crisis in Galilee; and, in this case, the news was bad. On the 16th of April, Bonaparte totally defeated the Ottoman army in the celebrated battle of Mount Tabor (the site of the Transfiguration of Christ). They captured all the Ottoman artillery, standards, and ammunition while the remains of the defeated army fled in confusion behind Mount Tabor. Finding their retreat by the Bridge of Jacob cut off, they rushed in desperation, in the night, through the deep waters of the Jordan, where great numbers were drowned.

A total dispersion followed this defeat, and no part of that army ever returned to challenge the French. Now that their rear was thus completely secured, their victorious troops returned to Acre to resume the siege with greater vigor than ever. The besieged were stunned by the news of the disastrous Ottoman defeat. In case anyone behind the walls should doubt that the calamity had occurred, the French exhibited the trophies and standards of the defeated army, including, above all, the crescent and three tails of the Pasha of Damascus.

Bonaparte had found time to conclude a sort of alliance with the Druses and other Christian tribes in the mountains of Syria, who only awaited the capture of Acre to declare openly for his cause. He addressed a proclamation to all the Christian tribes of Syria, inviting them to join his standard, and throw off the cruel yoke of Ahmed al-Jazzar.

In reply, the Pasha and Sir Sidney—knowing how intense was the desire of the French of all ranks to return to France—caused numerous copies of a proclamation to be thrown from the walls of Acre. In them, they urged the soldiers to mutiny and desertion, and offered to convey safely to France, with their arms and effects, every soldier who would take advantage of the offer. Yet, such was the attachment of the men to their general, that not one of them did so, although Bonaparte said afterwards, that this alluring offer, "certainly shook some of them." [1]

Sir Sidney, at the same time, issued another proclamation, in his own name, to the Christian tribes of Syria urging them, "to trust to the faith of a Christian knight rather than to that of an unprincipled *renegado*."

In a counter-counter proclamation to the French army, Bonaparte answered the propaganda of Djezzar Pasha and Sir Sidney by declaring that "owing to the heat of the climate and the excitement of war, the English commodore had actually gone mad, and any further communication with him was, therefore, prohibited." [2]

This insulting reflection upon his sanity so enraged Sir Sidney that he sent a challenge to Bonaparte to meet him in a dual. To this the young French commander-in-chief, showing contempt for Smith's rank as well as the challenge itself, proudly replied: "If Sir Sidney will send Marlborough from his grave to meet me, I will think about it. In the meantime, if the gallant commodore wishes to display his personal prowess, I will neutralize a few yards of the beach, and send a tall grenadier, with whom he can run a tilt." [3]

Stung to the quick, and conscious that he could make no fitting reply, our "Christian knight," (as he had described

---

[1] Abbott, J. S. (1855). *The History of Napoleon Bonaparte* (Vol. 1). New York: Harper & Brothers. p. 221.

[2] Ibid. p. 221

[3] Ibid. p. 221

himself) was obliged, for the only time in his career, to swallow an affront in impotent rage and silence.

Commenting upon the crushing contempt of this reply to Sir Sidney's challenge, Sir Walter Scott said: "The scorn of this reply ought to have been mitigated, considering it was addressed to one, in consequence of whose dauntless and determined opposition, Bonaparte's favorite object had failed, and who was presently to compel him for the first time to an inglorious retreat." [1]

The operations of the siege went on with relentless energy day and night. The French artillery was now reinforced by three 24-pounders and six 18-pounders brought up by land from Jaffa, where French cruisers from Alexandria had transported them. They were at once mounted and a heavy fire opened on the vehemently contested northeast tower. Mines were run under the walls, and every possible resource was used to reduce that corner, but in vain.

The defense under Phélippeaux and Sir Sidney was no less determined or less skillful than the attack. External works in the fosse were erected to take the enemy in the flanks as they advanced to the attack; the mines of the besiegers were countermined, and frequent sorties made to delay their approaches and carry off their entrenching tools. In these desperate contests, both General Caffarelli, who commanded the French engineers, and Colonel Phélippeaux, who directed those of the defense, died.

An English writer has said: "In no other military effort upon record did the French display greater perseverance, or more desperate bravery. In every one of their attacks, they seemed to understand beforehand that destruction was to be the rule and escape the exception. With this predestination strong upon them, they went up to the breach coolly and

---

[1] Scott, W. (1855). *Life of Napoleon Bonaparte*. Edinburgh: Adam and Charles Black. p. 273.

regularly, and with as much nonchalance as if death were an unimportant part of their military evolutions." [1]

Under all these disadvantages, the French pushed their lines forward, making no less than nine desperate assaults, only to be repulsed each time with heavy losses. Whenever the French penetrated into the town, as they did several times, they found the streets and houses barricaded. The cries and shrieks of the women, who ran through the streets throwing, according to the custom of the country, dust in the air, excited the Janizaries and male inhabitants to a resistance so frenzied that only retreat saved the French from annihilation. In such confined places, it was simply impossible for them to either deploy or fight to any sort of advantage.

But the besieged, on the other hand, did not wait behind their walls and entrenchments for the assaults of the enemy. Led by Sir Sidney Smith, they made no less than *twelve* furious sorties against the French lines, generally with heavy columns supported by the fire of every gun that could be brought to bear. This brought on heavy battles, with correspondingly heavy losses.

In all, no less than *twenty-one* such attacks and counter-attacks were made on the two sides during the sixty days of warfare. That amounts to *one for every three days the siege lasted*—an example of continuous, desperate fighting, with scarcely a parallel in any siege in history.

Fortunately for Sir Sidney and his heroic garrison, the succor they had in vain looked for by land from Abdallah Pasha, reached them by sea. On the evening of May 7th, a large Turkish fleet, having 7,000 troops and much artillery and ammunition on board, appeared in the Bay of Acre.

The historian. Sir Archibald Alison, gives the following admirable account of the operations of the siege at this decisive period:

---

[1] Howard. p. 86.

Napoleon, calculating that this reinforcement could not be disembarked for at least six hours, resolved to anticipate its arrival by an assault during the night. For this, the division of Bon, at ten at night, drove the enemy from their exterior works. The artillery took advantage of that circumstance to approach to the counterscarp and batter the curtains. At daybreak, another breach in the ramparts was declared practicable, and an assault ordered. The division of Lannes renewed the attack on the tower, while General Rambaud led the column to the new breach. The grenadiers, advancing with the most heroic intrepidity, made their way to the summit of the rampart, and the morning sun displayed the tri-color flag on the outer angle of the tower.

The fire of the place was now sensibly slackened, while the besiegers, redoubling their boldness, were seen entrenching themselves, in the lodgments they had formed, with sand bags and dead bodies, the points of their bayonets only appearing above the bloody parapet.

The troops in the roads were embarked in the boats, and were pulling as hard as they could across the bay; but several hours must still elapse before they could arrive at the menaced point. In this extremity, Sir Sidney Smith landed the crews of the ships, and led them, armed with pikes, to the breach. The sight reanimated the courage of the Turks, who were beginning to quail under the prospect of instant death. Immediately a furious contest ensued: the besieged hurled down large stones on the assailants, who fired at them within half pistol-shot, the muzzles of the muskets touched each other and the spearheads of the standards were locked together. At length the desperate daring of the French yielded to the unconquerable firmness of the British, and the heroic valor of the Mussulman; the grenadiers were driven from the tower, and a body of Turks issuing from the gates attacked them in flank while they crossed the ditch, and drove them back with great loss to the trenches.

But while this success was gained in one quarter, ruin was impending in another. The division headed by Rambaud succeeded in reaching the summit of the rampart, and leaping down into the tower, attained the very garden of the Pasha's seraglio. Everything seemed lost; but at the critical moment, Sir Sidney Smith, at the head of a regiment of Janizaries, rushed to the spot. The progress of the assailants was stopped by a tremendous fire from the housetops, and the barricades which surrounded the seraglio; and at length the French who had penetrated so far, were cut off from the breach by which they had entered, and driven into a neighboring mosque where they owed their lives to the humane intercession of Sir Sidney Smith, while the remainder of the attacking column was expelled over the breach, with very great losses on both sides. [1]

Bonaparte, obstinate to very madness, gave two days rest to his troops, and then ordered another assault, which is thus eloquently pictured in Sir Sidney's official report to Lord Nelson:

A little before sunset, a massive column appeared advancing to the breach with solemn step. The Pasha's idea was not to defend the breach at this time, but rather to let a certain number of the enemy in, and then close with them according to the Turkish mode of war. The column thus mounted the breach unmolested, and descended from the rampart into the Pasha's garden, where in a very few minutes the bravest and most advanced among them lay headless

---

[1] Alison, A. (1860). *The History of Europe* (Vol. 4). Edinburgh: William Blackwood and Sons. p. 633-635.

corpses; the saber, with the addition of a dagger in the other hand, proving more than a match for the bayonet. The rest retreated precipitately; and the commanding officer, who was seen manfully encouraging his men to mount the breach, and who we have since learned to be General Lannes, was carried off wounded by a musket-shot. General Rambaud was killed... Bonaparte will, no doubt, renew the attack, the breach being, as above described, perfectly practicable for fifty men abreast: indeed, the town is not, nor ever has been, defensible, according to the rules of art, but according to every other rule it must and shall be defended; not that it is in itself worth defending, but we feel that it is through this breach Bonaparte means to march to further conquests. It is on the issue of this conflict that depends the opinion of the multitude of spectators on the surrounding hills, who wait only to see how it ends, to join the victors; and with such a reinforcement for the execution of his known projects, Constantinople, and even Vienna, must feel the shock." [1]

It will thus be seen that, even then, Sir Sidney fully realized the true nature of the contest in which he was engaged against the vast designs of Bonaparte. He knew that the loss or salvation of the miserable heap of ruins called Acre was but as dust in the balance in comparison with the moral effect of victory or defeat.

Despite his heavy losses, Bonaparte *still* refused to order a retreat. "The fate of the East," said he, "is in yonder fort; the fall of Acre is the object of my expedition; Damascus will be its first fruit." [2] Although the 7,000 Turkish men from the fleet had now landed, he resolved to make a final effort on the 10th of May, with the division of Kléber, which had just arrived from the Jordan, and, proud of its great victory at

---

[1] Howard. p. 90.
[2] Alison. p. 635.

Mount Tabor, eagerly demanded to be led to the assault. "If St. Jean d'Acre is not taken this evening," said one of the colonels, as he was marching at the head of his regiment to the assault, "be assured Venoux is slain." [1] He kept his word; the fortress held out, but he lay at the foot of the walls.

The summit of the breach was again attained; but a murderous fire was poured upon them from all sides and stopped the troops. In vain, other columns, and even the Guides of Napoleon, his last reserve, advanced to the attack. They were all repulsed with dreadful slaughter. Among those killed in this last assault were the heroic General Bon and many other officers.

Success being now hopeless, Bonaparte at last made preparations for a retreat, after sixty days of open trenches; a proclamation was issued to the troops announcing that their return to Egypt was required to withstand a descent which was threatened by a large Turkish army from the Island of Rhodes. The plague was in Acre and the army had caught the contagion at Jaffa. By persisting longer, Bonaparte was liable to weaken himself to such a degree as not to be able to repulse new enemies.

No event, including the retreat from Moscow, so deeply affected Bonaparte as the retreat from Acre. It had cost him 3,000 of his best troops, slain or dead of their wounds. The army had become infected with the plague, and his reputation for invincibility was ended.

But these disasters, great as they were to an army situated as his was, were not the real cause of his chagrin. It was the destruction of his dreams of Oriental conquest that distressed him most. Standing on the mount of Richard Coeur de Lion, on the evening of the fatal assault by Kléber's division, he said to his secretary, Bourrienne,

> Yes, Bourrienne, that miserable fort has indeed cost me dear; but matters have gone too far not to

---

[1] Ibid. p. 636.

make a last effort. If I succeed, as I trust I shall, I shall find in the town all the treasures of the Pasha, and arms for 30,000 men. I shall raise and arm all Syria, which at this moment unanimously prays for the success of the assault. I will march on Damascus and Aleppo; I will swell my army as I advance with the discontented in every country through which I pass; I will announce to the people the breaking of their chains, and the abolition of the tyranny of the pashas. Do you not see that the Druses wait only for the fall of Acre to declare themselves? Have I not been already offered the keys of Damascus? ... I will arrive at Constantinople with armed masses; overturn the empire of the Turks, and establish a new one in the East, which will fix my place with posterity; and perhaps I may return to Paris by Adrianople and Vienna, after having annihilated the house of Austria.[1]

Splendid as his situation afterward was, he never ceased to regret the throne that he relinquished when he retired from Acre, and repeatedly said of Sir Sidney Smith, *"that man made me miss my destiny."* Certainly two such strokes as Toulon and Acre might well cause him to pass the highest tribute, grudging though it may have been, that he ever paid to any of his opponents.

In the Memoirs of Napoleon Bonaparte, by Bourrienne, occur the following statements concerning the siege of Acre, and the character of Sir Sidney Smith:

At Jaffa we had sufficient artillery; at St. Jean d'Acre we had not. At Jaffa we had to deal only with a garrison left to itself; at St. Jean d'Acre we were opposed by a garrison strengthened by reinforcements of men and supplies, supported by the English fleet, and assisted by European science.[2]

---

[1] Ibid. p. 637.

[2] Bourrienne, L. A. (1895). *Memoirs of Napoleon Bonaparte* (Vol. 1). New York: Charles Scribner's Sons. P. 208.

Sir Sidney Smith was, beyond doubt, the man who did us the greatest injury.[1]

Much has been said concerning his communications with the General-in-Chief. The reproaches which the latter cast upon him for endeavoring to seduce the soldiers and officers of the army by tempting offers were the more singular, even if they were well-founded, inasmuch as these means are frequently employed by leaders in war. As to the embarking of French prisoners on board a vessel in which the plague existed, the improbability of the circumstance alone, but especially the notorious facts of the case, repelled this odious accusation. I observed the conduct of Sir Sidney Smith closely at the time, and I remarked in him a chivalric spirit, which sometimes hurried him into trifling eccentricities; but I affirm that his behavior towards the French was that of a gallant enemy. I have seen many letters, in which the writers informed him that they were very sensible of the good treatment which the French experienced when they fell into his hands. Let any one examine Sir Sidney's conduct before the Convention of El Arisch, and after its rupture, and then they can judge of his character. [2]

Before he quitted St. Jean d'Acre, Bonaparte determined to leave a terrible token of his presence—he overwhelmed the town with his cannon fire, and left it almost reduced to ashes. He then bent his course towards Jaffa where he arrived in two days' march, his columns marching along by the sea, harassed all the way by the fire of the English gun-boats, which Sir Sidney caused to pursue them closely.

---

[1] *Author's Note* — Sir Sidney Smith was the only Englishman besides the Duke of Wellington who ever defeated Bonaparte in military operations. Sir John Moore in Spain, and Lord Hood with his allied fleets and armies at Toulon, were each obliged by Napoleon to make precipitate retreats before his vigorous attacks.

[2] Bourrienne. p. 200-201.

Through fire, hardship and disease he had lost 4,000 men. He carried away with him 1,200 more wounded, while the garrison of Acre, and the crews of the British fleet were weakened by the loss of over 7,000 of their numbers from fire and disease.

In order to avoid the burning passage across the Desert with the field artillery, it was embarked at Jaffa; but the whole of it fell into the hands of Sir Sidney Smith, with many of the more seriously wounded similarly embarked. With tireless energy, Sir Sidney followed the movements of the retreating French army with the light vessels of his squadron, and harassed it incessantly until it re-entered Egypt, with not much over half the numbers with which it started.

So ended one of the most memorable sieges in history, in which both sides showed a heroism and constancy beyond all praise; and here may be recounted one more anecdote to illustrate Sir Sidney's coolness.

At a most critical moment in the siege he had warped the *Tigre* in shore as far as could possibly be done, in order to bring her guns to bear on the flanks of the assaulting columns of the enemy. It is related that,

> As Sir Sidney Smith was going over the ship's side to land and hasten to the breach, the first lieutenant and the master of the *Tigre* chose that unseasonable moment to serve him with a written protest against *'placing his majesty's ship in danger of being lost.'* To this the savior of Turkey calmly replied, 'Gentlemen, his majesty's ships are built on purpose to be placed in danger of being lost, whenever his majesty's service requires it, and of that the commanding officer is the best judge!'[1]

Coolly glancing over his too prudent, but now crest-fallen subordinates, he ordered them to their proper posts, to open

---

[1] Howard. p. 403-404.

fire on the enemy. Meanwhile he hastened ashore to the 'imminent, deadly breach' and its perilous encounters—in which he seemed to lead a charmed life. Strangely enough he was never seriously injured in the many close combats in which he always took a conspicuous part during this siege. Always fresh from his "tub" in his fine quarters on board the *Tigre*, clean-shaven, immaculate in linen and dress, this typical English officer and dauntless fighter would coolly advance into the trenches to repulse the assaults of the enemy, or to lead the even more perilous sorties against them.

When the Grand Seignior, at Constantinople, who was still suffering from the shock of the great defeat inflicted upon his armies at Mount Tabor, learned of the retreat of the French from Acre he was overcome with joy. He presented the messenger who bore the tidings with seven purses of gold containing 3,000 florins. He dispatched a special Tartar courier to Sir Sidney with an aigrette [1] and sable furs (similar to those bestowed on Lord Nelson for the victory of the Nile) worth 25,000 piastres, and afterwards conferred upon him the insignia of the Ottoman Order of the Crescent.

In England, there was tremendous enthusiasm, and Parliament passed a formal vote of thanks on behalf of the nation, to Sir Sidney, and the officers and men under his command.

A pension of one thousand pounds per annum was also voted to the commodore as a further testimonial to his great

---

[1] *Editor's Note* – Actually, the Sultan was a bit more generous than what the author might lead you to believe. Sir Sidney indeed received an aigrette, which is a kind of plume that's worn on a turban. It's just that Sir Sidney's was the Imperial Aigrette (called the Chalingk) and it was made entirely of diamonds. In addition, he received a firman and the Sultan's seal, which effectively gave him unlimited life and death authority over his subjects "in the sea of the Archipelago, and of his Asiatic provinces." Sir Sidney could exercise this power at any time, for any reason, by simply showing the seal and document. The seal and the aigrette were the same as the Sultan's, except for the wording of the inscription around them.

services. The City of London presented him with its freedom, and a sword valued at 100 guineas; and from the Turkey Company, he received another valued at 300 guineas.

CHAPTER SEVEN
FIRST EGYPTIAN CAMPAIGN: THE
BATTLE OF ABOUKIR

The retreat of Bonaparte from Acre and his arrival at Cairo early in June 1799 was quickly followed in July by the disembarkation of the long-expected Turkish army that had been assembling for many months on the Island of Rhodes. They arrived via a combination of British and Turkish ships, under the command of Sir Sidney Smith, and the troops under the command of Mustafa Pasha. The troops consisted of 18,000 well-armed and equipped janissaries, the best troops of the Grand Seignior (who had reluctantly allowed them to be drafted from the great garrison of Constantinople), and a large train of artillery.

They landed on the narrow, sandy peninsula of Aboukir, about five leagues [15 miles] from Alexandria. There was no opposition from Marmont, the governor of that city, who would not leave his entrenchments in the face of the formidable naval gunfire support Sir Sidney had set up to protect the Turkish invasion force.

No cavalry accompanied this army, as it was planned that Murad Bey would descend from Upper Egypt with at least 3,000 Mamelukes. He would skirt his way along the edge of the desert at some distance from the Nile, in order to conceal his movements, as well as to avoid contact with the French troops. The goal was for him join the army of Mustafa Pasha at Aboukir in undiminished strength. In accordance with this plan, the Ottoman commander-in-chief, having his army and materiel safely landed, quietly waited in his cantonments among the sand hills of Aboukir for the appearance of the Mamelukes.

Unfortunately, the passage of so large a force of men, even through the confines of the desert, swift and secret though it was, did not escape the vigilance of the scouting parties of Bonaparte's chasseurs and Arabian spies. The Citizen-General Murat headed off Murad Bey with a strong body of French cavalry, much strengthened by several fine batteries of horse-artillery. They met in the desert near the Lakes of Natron, and some distance west of the Great Pyramids of Ghizeh, as he was hastening to the rendezvous at Aboukir.

After a bloody hand-to-hand battle, the discipline of the European squadrons and batteries triumphed over the undisciplined masses and personal daring of the Mameluke horsemen. The Mamelukes sustained losses so severe that their chief was obliged to retrace his steps back into Upper Egypt, and take refuge in the Libyan Desert. There he was unable to make another attack in the brief time that elapsed before the French thunderbolt landed on the hapless Mustafa Pasha and his army at Aboukir.

Mustafa Pasha, however, encouraged by the powerful aid of the allied fleets at anchor in the Bay of Aboukir, and confident in the fighting power of his 18,000 fierce Janizaries, was filled with pride and self-confidence. He did not doubt that he would soon destroy the Infidel army and conquer Egypt again for his imperial master. After all, the Grand Seignior at Istanbul had chosen him, among all his servants, for his wisdom and courage to perform this most honorable mission.

Sir Sidney Smith had quickly taken the measure of this haughty fool of a pasha, but could do nothing to remedy the obvious danger of having such a commander for the Ottoman army. With the crisis so near at hand and Istanbul so far away, there was no way he could have obtained a more suitable appointment.

In his letters to Murad Bey, Mustafa Pasha had highly offended the heroic Mameluke prince, by his vainglorious boastings that, "A very different fate would meet the Infidel dogs of Franks from that which had followed the numerous contests of the Mamelukes with them, if they ever dared to appear before him and his invincible Janizaries!"

"Pasha," exclaimed the indignant Murad Bey, in his reply, "render thanks to the Prophet that they have not appeared, for when they do you will vanish like dust before them." It was a prediction that was so literally and awfully fulfilled that it must have given a shock to Murad Bey himself, despite his anger towards the conceited Pasha.

When the Mamelukes were forced to retreat back into the desert, there was then nothing left to oppose Bonaparte but the Turkish army.

The Turks were well supplied with artillery, and encamped behind two lines of entrenchments extending nearly across the neck of the Aboukir peninsula. Sir Sidney Smith placed his gunboats at either end of the Turkish lines, in the sea or in Lake Maadieh, in order to strengthen the defense as much as possible. His larger ships could not approach close enough to take part in the battle.

This was the position of Mustafa's army when Bonaparte suddenly appeared at 6 o'clock in the morning of July 25, 1799, with only 6,000 of his veterans. They, however, included the cavalry and flying artillery that had just beaten Murad Bey. The French advanced in a sudden rush upon the surprised Turks in the first lines of entrenchments.

The Turks panicked and rushed into the sea in crowds, preferring an uncertain death there to certain death on land.

In this terrible battle, quarter was neither asked nor expected on either side. The French well remembered the cruel fate of the garrison of the Castle of Aboukir, three hundred in number, which the Turks had stormed immediately after landing and massacred to a man—cutting off the heads of the dead and wounded alike.

Sir Sidney hastened on shore to lend his personal aid to Mustafa Pasha, but the terror and disorder had become so great there was nothing he could do. Amid the surging disordered masses that nearly trampled him under foot, he was unable even to make his way to the headquarters of the Pasha. Meanwhile the rapid and daring advance of the French had so mixed the two armies that the English gun-boats, who were supposed to rake the flanks of the attacking enemy, had to cease firing lest they should slaughter their own allies. This was of great help to the French, who quickly opened a well-directed fire from the heavy guns mounted in the captured Turkish lines upon the lightly armed allied gun-boats, thus forcing them to withdraw entirely from firing-range.

The remains of Mustafa Pasha's first lines had collapsed back upon his second, and the bulk of the Turkish infantry, now stripped of its artillery and having no cavalry to support it, were driven into a narrow space along the shore of Aboukir Bay. The furious charges of the Republican cavalry under Murat, and the murderous onslaughts of the infantry, drove the huge masses of Turks headlong into the sea. Over twelve thousand of them perished in a hopeless attempt to wade and swim to their ships, more than a mile distant.

While these fierce charges of Bonaparte's cavalry and infantry continued, the English and Turkish naval officers were able to witness, through their glasses, every detail of the spectacle. They saw several batteries of Napoleon's famous horse-artillery, fully mounted and drawn by powerful grey Arabian stallions, suddenly dash forward to the seashore at their utmost speed. Across the sand hills they pressed, amid clouds of yellow dust. With marvelous quickness and a machine-like precision, they swung into line of battle, halted, unlimbered and opened with a devastating storm of grape-shot at the very heels of the retreating Janizaries. They were so close, indeed, that the red tongues of flame, flashing through the white smoke of the guns, seemed literally to burn their way into the disordered masses, while driving them still further into the deep waters where they soon sunk to their deaths.

Dreading the chances of death in the sea less than the terrors of further butchery upon the land, a beaten, terror-stricken army was literally committing suicide. The tragic suddenness of the French attack appalled the stoutest hearts among the horrified on-lookers of the allied fleets. They realized that a catastrophe was about to happen, and yet were powerless to do anything.

Four thousand Turks were slain on the land, desperately fighting to the last. About two thousand more fled to the Castle of Aboukir at the extreme end of the peninsula. Two or three days later, when the sight of 12,000 Turkish bodies floating in the bay had somewhat softened French hearts, they were allowed to surrender.

The proud Mustafa Pasha had been captured by a squad of Republican cavalry who dashed into the very centre of his camp. In despair, Mustafa fired at and slightly wounded Murat. Murat, in return, with a stroke of his saber, cut off two of his fingers and sent him prisoner to Bonaparte.

Bonaparte courteously offered to send a letter to Mustafa's imperial master at Istanbul, outlining the courage he had shown in the battle; but he was repulsed by the proud Turk with the haughty reply: "Thou mayest save thyself that trouble! My master knows me better than thou canst!" [1]

The small army of the victors, whose losses had been surprisingly light, was actually burdened by the captured trophies. There were standards, cannon, small arms,

[1] Abbott. p. 235

ammunition, tents, and supplies of every sort, which had been landed in vast quantities by the allied fleets.

The rout of his Ottoman allies had been so sudden, the disorder and peril so great, that our commodore managed his own escape only with the utmost difficulty. The boat that was awaiting him from the *Tigre* was nearly overwhelmed by drowning Janizaries, as they each struggled for a few moments in the agonies of death. The English seamen, after obeying Sir Sidney's humane command to take on board as many as possible, rowed with all their might to escape the deadly hail of shot from the hostile batteries. In addition, they had to pull away from the sea of despairing faces and outstretched hands of those they could not save. As their hapless wearers disappeared beneath the waves, their big, red-plumed turbans remained floating on the surface of the sea, bobbing up and down, like some vast bed of flowers agitated by the wind.

Such was the unparalleled battle in which, for one of the few times in the annals of war, a hostile army was utterly and completely destroyed.[1] Except for the crews of the Turkish

---

[1] *Author's Note* — Several writers, apparently, with the idea of detracting as much as possible from this astonishing victory of Bonaparte's, have greatly reduced the numbers of the Ottoman army at Aboukir, to as low as 8,000 or 9,000 men.

Not only are they at variance with many of the best and most accurate authorities, who give the numbers as 18,000 and even more, but a moment's consideration would show that the landing of so small a force as 9,000 men anywhere in Egypt would simply have been to consign it to certain destruction. Not only would 9,000 men have been totally inadequate to invade Egypt, but also such an attempt would have argued a lack of sense and judgment on the part of both the English and Turkish cabinets. They fully understood the difficulties of such an enterprise, and did, in fact, assemble 20,000 men on the Island of Rhodes to undertake it. They, in fact, disembarked 18,000 of this army with a large train of artillery, which was also to have been reinforced, as we have seen, by 3,000 Mameluke horsemen. Only those kinds of numbers would have allowed them to take the field in sufficient strength to have a fair chance of success.

transports and ships of war, Sir Sidney's allies had completely vanished.

A profound silence had followed the clamor, noise, and confusion of the battle so that, as he ascended the sides of his flagship that fatal evening, he could scarcely believe what he had just witnessed.

A melancholy night was passed on board the allied fleets. Numerous volunteer boat crews returned with empty boats to their waiting ships, after vain efforts to rescue their comrades. There were none remaining to rescue, or, indeed, ever to return, except those who would rise in two days time from the depths of Aboukir Bay.

Sounds of grief and loud lamentations burst from the frenzied Turks gathered on the decks of their ships. "Oh! Allah! Allah! The Faithful have this day perished in thy sight, and thine Hand was not lifted to save them! Tonight thy servants sleep beneath the waves, while the proud Infidels are resting in their tents, and trailing thy standards in the dust! Woe! Thrice woe, is Islam this day!" [1]

A frightful, uncanny sight was presented to the English and Turkish fleets when on the third day the bloated bodies of the drowned soldiers suddenly rose by the thousands to the surface of the sea, directly among the ships still riding at anchor, as if appealing to be taken on board again. It was too much even for the iron-nerve of the English, who quickly weighed their anchors and sailed round to the front of the harbor of Alexandria, and joined the rest of their small blockading squadron.

Meanwhile, the Turkish warships, and their immense fleet of transports, tenantless now, and without any further reason to remain on the coast of Egypt, spread their sails and fled this scene of horror, overwhelmed with grief and despair.

---

[1] Editor's Note — This citation could not be located in any available text. It is believed the author was using a bit of "artistic license" here and not actually making a quotation.

Mustafa Pasha's dead Janizaries, however, remained behind in Aboukir Bay, as their comrades-in-arms sailed away. Swinging back and forth with the waves, they began a slow, solemn movement back to the beach from which they had so recently fled. It was as though they wanted to avenge their wild panic by landing again to renew once more the battle they had just lost. It was a last assault of the dead.

Fearless now of hostile bayonet or battery, unheralded by beat of drum or blare of brazen-throated trumpet—those ghastly battalions, with voiceless lips and weaponless hands, impelled by the tides and the winds, threw themselves blindly forward with the white breakers upon Aboukir's fatal strand. In long, broken lines and formless masses, advancing and receding, rising and falling, with the restless waves, their confused jostling caused aimless blows and the faint rattle of steel from the scabbards of undrawn sabers. The sounds would cease, suddenly, as the wearers drifted apart.

There were dull, meaningless shocks and strange noises amid the hollow roar of the sea, which were more terrible than any living tumult of battle. There were assaults that do not cease with the coming of darkness; that were more persistent and determined than those of the bravest columns; that were heedless of repulses. They were now invincible regiments, reinforced by more corpses with every wave. They pressed onward—ever pressing onward—till they rested in tangled heaps at the foot of those low, sandy heights. They will hold firm, this time—yet, only to rot and fester beneath the burning rays of an Egyptian mid-summer sun. They would become the prey of the beaks and claws of countless vultures that tear at bloodless lips and sightless eyes.

The French troops were conscious of the health danger from the thousands of corpses. They made a great effort, with the enforced help of the Arabs who had flocked to the scene to plunder the bodies, to bury as many of the dead as they could. This had to be done during the brief time it was possible to approach or touch them, by throwing them into long trenches hastily hollowed out of the hot, dry sands. Vast numbers of bodies could not be buried, however, and the horrible odors from decaying flesh and bones poisoned the air and waters of Aboukir Bay throughout the remainder of that year. All except the beasts and birds of prey shunned the beach.

The morning after the battle, Bonaparte sent a flag-of-truce to the Turkish fleet that, under the pretext of exchanging prisoners, was an attempt to obtain some news from Europe. Sir Sidney Smith stopped this messenger, and had him come on board the *Tigre*. He treated him very well and learned, among other things, that the French in Egypt were ignorant of the long train of disasters to the Republic in Italy and Germany. Indeed, they had heard nothing from Europe for the past ten months, owing to the strict blockade. So, Smith indulged in the "courtesy" of sending to the French headquarters a quantity of the latest European newspapers. This made Bonaparte and the French army acquainted with the disasters experienced by the Executive Directory in Europe—the loss of Italy, the reverses in the Alps, the retreat of Massena to Zurich, the capture of Corfu by the Russians and English, and the close blockade of Malta which promised soon to fall to the British.

However, the propaganda ploy had an unexpected result. If Sir Sidney Smith might be said to have made Napoleon miss his destiny at Acre, he might also, by this act at Alexandria, be said to have contributed directly to his rise in France. As soon as he read about the situation at home, Napoleon decided to return. He arrived at the very moment to be elevated to supreme power, when the Republic was *in extremis* under the assaults of the European allies. His coming, if it had been delayed by even a few months, would have been too late!

Bonaparte had secretly made all his preparations to escape by sea, and his small squadron of two frigates and two xebecs lay in readiness to slip out of the harbor at the first opportunity. He knew his ships could not force their way past the British, so he waited until the blockading fleet might leave the way open by having to depart station for one reason or another.

Of course, Sir Sidney had no suspicion that this escape plan was in place. If he had, nothing could have induced him to relax his vigilance. The capture of Bonaparte would have been of greater importance than the mightiest victory; and would, besides, have been a balm to his wounded pride in the matter of the personal challenge at Acre. Indeed, just by looking at the remnants of the French fleet shut up in the harbor of Alexandria, there was no reason to suppose that a dash of any sort would occur.

At this very time it also chanced, unfortunately for Sir Sidney, that his ships had all run short of water and it was absolutely necessary to sail across to the Island of Cyprus for a fresh supply. No water could be procured on the desert coast of Egypt because all the ports and both mouths of the Nile were in enemy hands. They also needed to repair some damage done to the *Theseus* by an accidental explosion of some sixty langridge shells, captured from the French vessels taken near Jaffa during the retreat from Syria. Accordingly, he sailed for Cyprus, intending to return with all speed, leaving only one brig to watch the Alexandria harbor.

Thus, the way out was left unguarded for a few days, and Bonaparte was able to set sail for France. He was too far advanced along the African coast to be overhauled; and, without knowing for sure that Napoleon was on board, the commodore could not have quit the blockade along the Egyptian coast.

As might be imagined, Smith's chagrin was extreme when he learned what had happened. However, he was not a man to nurse regrets; and, therefore, resumed the duties of his blockade.

CHAPTER EIGHT
THE CONVENTION OF EL ARISCH

The sudden return of Bonaparte to Europe took the French army completely by surprise, and produced the utmost discontent and discouragement in all ranks, from the new commander-in-chief, General Kléber, on down. M. Poussielgue, the civil administrator of Egypt, prepared a report on the state of the colony. It was filled with gross misrepresentations, stating that the army was reduced to half its numbers and could not muster 15,000 men, and that it was in such destitution from the lack of arms, ammunition, clothing, and money that it could no longer defend the country.

These dispatches and a great number of letters from officers of the army, full of despair, were taken at sea by the English cruisers and sent to the English government. The government immediately published them all, and the cabinet accepted them as factual. This led the cabinet into a series of serious errors.

In this despondent frame of mind, General Kléber sent one of his officers to make overtures of peace to the Grand-Vizier of Turkey, who was marching through

Palestine at the head of a very large army. Through the influence of Sir Sidney Smith, Kléber's proposals met with a favorable reception.

As all the letters intercepted by the English cruisers showed, the French had an ardent desire to return home. To play on this desire, Sir Sidney conceived the idea of getting General Kléber to sign an honorable treaty for the immediate evacuation of Egypt. Further, it was designed to ship the French army back to France before the French Directory could either give or refuse its consent to such an arrangement.

Kléber knew that the return of his army to Europe would only be possible with the concurrence of the British, so General Desaix and M. Poussielgue went on board Sir Sidney's flagship to conduct the initial negotiations. Sir Sidney hoped to work out most of the details of the treaty before he and the French officers contacted the Grand-Vizier, who was then encamped with his army at Gaza, not far from the Egyptian frontier fortress of El Arisch.

Sir Sidney, delighted at having the opportunity to get to know, in a social way, so distinguished a member of the French army as General Desaix, treated him with special courtesy. A keen military observer, General Desaix, quickly recognized and expressed his admiration for the excellent order and discipline among the crew of the British battleship—to the evident pleasure and pride of his host.

The pretensions and demands initially put forth by both parties necessarily prolonged the negotiations. One after another, however, the inadmissible claims were eliminated; and an agreement was, at last, reached, with good feeling on both sides.

The negotiations had gone on for a fortnight on board the *Tigre* while floating at the pleasure of the winds off the coasts of Syria, Cyprus, and Egypt. This was a strange corner of the southeastern Mediterranean, the shores of which were a desert just as it had been in the days of Solomon the Magnificent, and as far back as human history extends.

Of little value in itself, this desert strip and isthmus has, because of its location as a sort of bridge between the continents of Asia and Africa, been a battleground of nations from the most remote antiquity. Here, in battles whose slaughter dyed its yellow sands red, Egypt sought to halt and beat back the vast tides of Asiatic invasion, only to be overwhelmed at last.

The face of this strip, often visible to the negotiators from the decks of the *Tigre*, has remained as completely unchanged, perhaps, as any known portion of the earth's surface. It is as difficult to cross today, as it was when the parched legions of Sesostris, of Cambyses, of Alexander, and of Bonaparte, in turn, toiled through its desolate, burning wastes.

Finally, the participation of the Grand-Vizier was needed, so Sir Sidney proposed that he go to Gaza, the headquarters of the Vizier, to arrange a cease-fire and to prepare for the coming of the French representatives. The French agreed. Sir Sidney landed and ordered the captain of the *Tigre* to meet him at Jaffa where General Desaix and M. Poussielgue with their staffs were to be landed if the Grand-Vizier agreed to negotiate.

Sir Sidney became fearful for the safety of the French officers when he saw the semi-barbarous hordes of the Grand-Vizier fighting among themselves over their provisions, or for the possession of a well. Although he was given assurance of their safety, he insisted that their tents be pitched in the Grand-Vizier's quarter of the camp, and that a guard of chosen men from the Vizier's own guards be posted about these tents. Finally, he caused his own tents to be pitched beside them, and brought a detachment of English seamen to protect both himself and the French officers that were entrusted to his honor from all violence.

Amid the sand hills near the seashore at Jaffa, General Desaix and M. Poussielgue saw, with a shudder of horror, the immense pyramid of the bleaching bones and skulls of what had been the Turkish garrison of Jaffa, some 4,000 in number. They had been captured the year before at the storming of that town by the French army and Bonaparte had them shot. [1] This was done because he knew that the Turks respected no parole given to Infidels, and that if liberated would at once rejoin the other Turkish forces to fight him as fiercely as ever. Napoleon could not leave enemy forces in his rear, and his first responsibility was to secure the safety of his small army.

This ghastly memorial of the Syrian expedition, the goals of which were ended at Acre by Sir Sidney Smith, was only too well calculated to incite the vengeance of Mussulman fanatics upon any Frenchmen who chanced to come within reach. Therefore, it was with great pleasure the French negotiators saw the bayonets of the English marines that had been ordered by Sir Sidney to escort them by land from Jaffa to Gaza, and to guard their encampment while there.

---

[1] Actually, it was even more brutal than that. On March 7, 1799 Napoleon captured and ransacked the town of Jaffa. They killed everyone they encountered, be they civilian or military, including 2000 soldiers who were trying to surrender. Another 2500 soldiers took refuge in the local fort. After officially and formally surrendering, the French army killed every one of them in a two-day massacre as follows. "We are told by Buonaparte's own commissary Miot, who was on the spot, that the Jaffa prisoners were marched into the midst of a vast square, formed by the French troops, into which the silent column of victims were driven in fearful confusion, foreseeing their fate; but that 'they shed no tears; they uttered no cries; some who were wounded and could not march so fast as the rest, were bayoneted on the way.' The others were halted near a pool of stagnant and dirty water, divided into small bodies, marched to different parts, and there fusilladed. He adds, 'Our soldiers had exhausted their cartridges, and it was necessary to destroy those prisoners remaining, with the bayonet and the sword.'" (Barrow. p. 164)

It is no wonder that Desaix and Poussielgue were a tad nervous about visiting the Ottoman camp.

Thus well protected they reached Gaza, admiring, *en route*, the magnificent grove of very ancient olive trees that forms an avenue several miles long north of the city. The town itself, they found, stood upon an isolated hill about a hundred feet high, surrounded by ruinous walls. The French officers found their large, handsome tents pitched, very agreeably in the shade of some scattered palms, olive and orange trees, not far from the site of the famed Gate of Gaza. This was the place where the mighty Samson, "Took the doors of the gate of the city, and the two posts, and went away with them, bar and all, and put them upon his shoulders, and carried them up to the top of an hill that is before Hebron." (Judges 16:3) [1]

While "the hill looking towards Hebron," was indeed still there, the battering left by the French artillery was, also, very much in evidence, and again reminded everyone of the ravages the French had inflicted only the year before. Nevertheless, the French officers were well received by the Grand-Vizier, Jouseff Pasha. They took up their quarters in the midst of the Ottoman hosts, which were encamped in irregular fashion around Gaza in cornfields and vineyards that were interspersed and adorned by hedges of cactus. This was possibly the very same ground where Samson is also reputed to have performed his celebrated feat of catching 300 foxes, tying their tails together and putting "a fire-brand in the midst between two tails," then setting fire to them. After that, he turned them loose in the ripened cornfields and vineyards of Gaza, with disastrous results for the Gazites.

---

[1] *Author's Note* - To the south of Gaza is a remarkable hill, quite isolated and bare, with a small mosque and a graveyard on the summit. It is variously called El Muntar, "The Watch-tower", "The Mount of Samson", and "The Hill of Hebron", and is supposed to be the same mountain "before (or facing) Hebron" to which Samson carried the gates of Gaza.

To the east of the city is the Tomb of Samson, and the remains of a racecourse, the corners marked by granite shafts with Greek inscriptions on them.

The camp of the Grand-Vizier presented one of the strangest sights that could be conceived—of large striped tents, bright with heavy fringe and banners, crowds of servants in dresses of every color, and numerous fine horses, camels, and dromedaries, richly caparisoned, ready for immediate use. 15,000 camels had been hired from the Arabs to aid in the transport of the army and its supplies to Egypt, and presented a stupendous sight.

The foreign negotiators were surprised at seeing several large carriages, hung on springs after the European fashion. An even more interesting sight, however, soon presented itself. Near the Vizier's tent were twelve large wooden palanquins, carved and gilded, richly furnished and curtained with silken draperies of the brightest hues. In each, there was a pretty, young, harem girl, whose society the Grand-Vizier had felt to be indispensable to alleviate the discomforts and fatigues of the campaign. The breeze, blowing toward the foreign tents from those of the harem, was scented with the perfumes of aloes and attar of roses.

Needless to say, whatever precautions the Grand-Vizier took to insure the safety of the foreign officers, they were, in fact, trifling, compared with those adopted to protect his harem. He had a crowd of armed eunuchs and quadrupled guards of his most ferocious janissaries, to safeguard that part of his encampment from intrusion. Alas, all hopes of introductions to the harem maidens had to be forgotten, if indeed they were ever entertained.

After long discussion, it was agreed that hostilities should cease for ninety days: that the French army should evacuate Egypt, yield up to the Turkish troops the fortresses in the eastern part of the country, at stated intervals, and relinquish Cairo in forty days. That the French army and all its civilian attendants should be transported back to Europe in vessels furnished by Turkey, with all their arms, artillery, effects, etc., and receive 3,000,000 francs to meet their expenses, during the time the evacuation was going forward. In addition, Sir Sidney Smith engaged in his own name, and in the name of the Russian commissioner, to furnish the French army with passports, which would prevent them from molestation from English or Russian cruisers.

General Desaix was opposed to the evacuation of Egypt under any conditions, and refused to sign this celebrated convention—named in honor of the frontier fortress of El Arisch. He said he needed an express order from Kléber as commander-in-chief, and sent his aide-de-camp, Savary, (afterwards made a general and Duke of Rovigo by the Emperor Napoleon) to Kléber's headquarters at Salahieh, where he was preparing to oppose the Turkish invasion of Egypt.

The latter, sharing the ardent desire of nearly all the French army to return to France under almost any honorable conditions, at once gave the order to Desaix to sign the Convention of El Arisch, and sent Savary back to Gaza with it. General Kléber also charged Savary to obtain the French wife of a sergeant killed at El Arisch, whom he knew to have been given to a pasha upon the capture of that fort and massacre of its garrison by the Turks a short time before. He was desirous, he said, not to leave behind a single individual belonging to the French army.

Savary says: "On arriving at the Turkish advanced post, I received an escort which conducted me to the Vizier's tent, round which were strewed the bodies of wretches who had been put to death during the day. I found Sir Sidney with the Vizier, and seized that opportunity to claim the woman I have mentioned. I then learned from the Vizier that he himself had given her to the Pasha of Jerusalem; but he said he would ask for her back, and immediately send her on to us. I went thence with Sir Sidney Smith to General Desaix's tent, where the treaty was signed on the night of my arrival."[1]

The Vizier then made known to his good friend, the Pasha of Jerusalem, his desire for, as well as the importance of, the

---

[1] Savary, A. J. (1828). *Memoirs of the Duke of Rovigo* (Vol. 1). London: Henry Colburn. p. 136.

immediate return of his fair captive to her countrymen. However, this request soon developed into a most complicated state of affairs. Far from being a forlorn "captive," this young and pretty French widow, with the guile and the arts of all widowhood, had already completely fascinated and enslaved that unsophisticated oriental personage, the Pasha of Jerusalem, and was unwilling to abandon the rich conquest she had made.

Soon after the convention was signed, Sir Sidney and General Desaix took leave of each other on very friendly terms, and parted on good terms with the Grand-Vizier by whom they had been handsomely entertained and treated.

Savary further relates that:

> Just as General Desaix, with his staff and escort, was about to start on his return through the desert to Egypt, a letter was brought to him from Jerusalem; it was from the captive widow, who thanked him for the interest he had shown in her fate, but declared that she did not wish to take advantage of it, as she found herself extremely well off, and very handsomely used by the Pasha, and, therefore, was resolved to remain where she was: she wished us success and a happy journey. [1]

> At a later period, this female sutler became the protectress of the Christian establishments in Syria, to which she rendered important services. She was of use to us in the time of the Consulate, and was provided with the means for supporting the ascendancy she had acquired. [2]

Sir Sidney Smith returned to Jaffa and went on board the *Tigre*, justly proud of the splendid diplomatic victory he had won. Without the sacrifice of a single life, the vast designs of Bonaparte would be completely frustrated, France finally

---

[1] Ibid. p. 136-137.

[2] Ibid. p. 137

driven from Egypt and the East, and all would return to the way it was before the invasion. Above all, it relieved Great Britain from the strain and losses of having to continue hostilities in that remote region. He was also aware that this triumph was due to the fact that his own vigilance had enabled him to open negotiations at the moment of greatest despondency in the French army—that following Bonaparte's sudden departure for Europe.

In Egypt Kléber immediately prepared for the evacuation, to the great joy of the army. The Grand-Vizier advanced, and the French handed over to him, consecutively, the fortresses of Katieh, Salahieh, and Belbeis, while Kléber directed the troops to march to Alexandria and Rosetta, where they would embark.

At the same time, the English cabinet had received notice of the overtures made by Kléber to the Grand-Vizier and Sir Sidney Smith for the evacuation of Egypt. Having in its possession Kléber's false report to the Directory of the condition of the French army in Egypt, the English cabinet rejected the treaty. After all, the French were an army whose situation was represented as hopeless by its commander to his own government. So, they dispatched an order to Lord Keith, the new commander-in-chief of the British Mediterranean fleet, not to grant any conditions to General Kléber except an unconditional surrender of his army as prisoners of war. The relay of these orders did not reach Sir Sidney Smith till about the 20th of February 1800, to whom they caused the deepest embarrassment.

He had acted without precise instructions from his government, because he believed his authority was sufficient, and that his action would be approved. He was better acquainted than the government at home with the reality of things in Egypt and the actual strength of the French army. He also knew General Kléber would never surrender himself as a prisoner of war. With bitter disappointment, he saw the Convention of El Arisch, which he had so skillfully managed to wring from a momentary weakness in the enemy, wholly set aside.

He instantly wrote to Kléber, however, to express his mortification, to inform him of what had happened, and to advise him to suspend the delivery of any more fortresses to the Grand-Vizier. He told him to wait for fresh orders from England before he took any other steps.

General Kléber at once acted upon this most honorable warning. He stopped the evacuation, recalled his troops to Cairo, and gave notice to the Grand-Vizier to suspend his march otherwise he would renew hostilities. The Grand-Vizier replied that the Convention of El Arisch was signed; that it must be honored; and, therefore, that he would continue to advance upon Cairo.

General Desaix had already departed for France, upon the belief that a treaty had been signed. But in a letter to M. Poussielgue Sir Sidney said: "...It would only be throwing out a snare to my brave antagonists, were I to encourage them to embark. I owe it to the French army, and to myself, to acquaint them with the state of things, which, however, I am endeavoring to change. At any rate, I stand between them and the false impressions that have dictated a proceeding of this kind. ... I then propose, sir, that you should come on board, in order to consult on what is to be done in the difficult circumstances in which we are placed. I view with calmness the heavy responsibility to which I am subject; my life is at stake—I know it; but I should prefer an unmerited death to the preservation of my existence by exposing both my life and honor." [1]

Napoleon himself was fully sensible of Sir Sidney's noble course upon this occasion, and said: "He manifested great honor in sending immediately to Kléber the refusal of Lord Keith to ratify the treaty, *which saved the French army*. If he had kept it secret for seven or eight days longer, Cairo would

---

[1] Howard. p. 117.

have been given up to the Turks, and the French army would necessarily have been obliged to surrender to the English. He also showed great humanity and honor in all his proceedings toward the French who fell into his hands." [1]

There was a great deal of grandeur in Sir Sidney's conduct. The temptation must have been great to remain silent. This would have been increased by the fact that it would not have been a treachery of *his* doing, but merely watching one be done by others. In addition, it would remove an army of nearly 30,000 tried veterans from the ranks of his country's enemies. Yet, he did not hesitate to follow the dictates of his own high sense of honor by giving instant notice of danger to his foes.

Being informed of the ultimatums going back-and-forth between Kléber and the Grand-Vizier, Sir Sidney hurriedly sent agents to get between them and try to smooth things over. They said that full explanations had already been sent to London, which would certainly cause the Convention of El Arisch to be ratified. Given that fact, he urged them to suspend hostilities and wait.

To this both parties consented in principle, but stipulated conditions that were mutually unacceptable. The Grand-Vizier insisted that Cairo should be surrendered to him, and Kléber that the Vizier should fall back to the frontier. It was a deadlock from which fighting was, ultimately, the only possible recourse.

The Grand-Vizier thereupon resumed his advance, and on the 19th of March 1800, the two armies met on the plain of Koubbe, a few miles east of Cairo, in the famed battle of Heliopolis. Kléber with only 12,000 French veterans completely defeated the Ottoman army—70,000 strong—slaying over 8,000, and capturing many thousands of prisoners. All of its artillery, baggage and tents, were captured, including the twelve gilded harem palanquins of

---

[1] Abbott. p. 226.

the Grand-Vizier, and his European carriages. The dazzling occupants of harem palanquins, it is to be feared, fell into rude hands—a rare and most luscious spoil of war in this short campaign. Certain articles of risqué oriental clothing were also taken with the harem, the singularity of which produced shouts of laughter among the troops. The French rested from several days of plunder at the edge of the desert east of Salahieh, into whose sandy wastes the remains of the enemy had been driven to perish of hunger and thirst.

In a few days, the French had recovered all the fortresses, their garrisons surrendering without resistance. The remains of the great Turkish army had retreated to Gaza, from whence it had originally advanced with all the pride of apparently irresistible military strength. The defeated army, after losing great numbers from hunger and thirst, then suffered from attacks of hostile Arabs, who plundered the disorganized troops. To complete their misfortunes the plague broke out, and nearly destroyed what few men were left. The Grand-Vizier, with great difficulty, effected his own escape at the head of only 500 horsemen.

This battle was, in truth, one of the most disastrous the Ottoman Empire ever sustained; and the Turks held that the timely warning given by Sir Sidney Smith to General Kléber was the cause of it. They never forgave him.

The great victory of Heliopolis completely restored French affairs in Egypt. Its spoils, together with the contributions levied on the rebellious inhabitants of Cairo and other towns, and the immense booty taken in that battle by the soldiers for their personal use, placed the army in the greatest affluence and comfort. The troops returned to their quarters joyous and triumphant. In addition, having learned that Bonaparte had become First Consul, they felt no doubt he would speedily send reinforcements and everything else that was needed. As a result, Kléber abandoned all thoughts of giving up Egypt, and set in motion many plans to improve his position, as well as the condition of the country itself.

In the midst of his great designs, an obscure fanatic, Suleiman al-Halabi, of Aleppo, assasinated General Kléber. He asserted that he was inspired by Allah to slay the enemy of the Prophet and of the Grand Seignior, who had slaughtered such numbers of the True Believers at Heliopolis. He also confessed at his trial that he had been further incited to the act by the Aga of Janizaries at Gaza, who furnished him with a dromedary and money to go to Cairo. Under the mask of presenting a petition for charity, he accosted the General when walking in the gardens of the palace. While Kléber was in the act of reading it, the assassin drew a dagger, twenty inches in length, and rapidly stabbed him in five different places Kléber sunk to the earth mortally wounded. [1]

The skeleton of Suleiman al-Halabi, who was, of course, put to death for his crime, was sent to Paris and may be seen there in the *Musée de l'Homme* in Paris. The bones of the right arm, in particular, are perfectly black. [2]

Upon Kléber's death, General Menou, who had been appointed second in command by Bonaparte at the same time he made Kléber commander-in-chief, assumed command in Egypt. Menou declined all steps towards an accommodation, and rejected the new overtures of the Grand-Vizier, who dared not return to Constantinople to face the enraged Grand Seignior. Now, much humbled by his disastrous defeat at the battle of Heliopolis, he hastened to make his overtures filled with profuse expressions of his amicable sentiments.

---

[1] *Editor's Note* — It should be noted that there are several different versions of exactly how the assassination was conducted, how many times Kléber was stabbed, the type of knife used, and so forth. Parson's account, presented here, includes all the major elements noted by others, and is probably as good an account as any.

[2] *Editor's Note* — The bones are black because, after his arrest, he was tortured and his right arm was burned to the bone. He was eventually executed by impalement, which, it might be imagined, the French assumed was a good old-fashioned Ottoman way of doing it.

Sir Sidney Smith, whose explanations and clarifications had been received in London, was now empowered by his government to carry into effect the Convention of El Arisch. The British government had at last recognized the falsity of Kléber's intercepted dispatches to the French Directory and had hastened to send fresh instructions to Lord Keith at Minorca. They countermanded their former orders not to allow the passage of the French army, except as prisoners of war, as well as ratifying all the terms of the convention itself. By this time, however, it was too late. The French were now determined to keep Egypt.

Sir Sidney's actions in negotiating the Convention of El Arisch were at first severely criticized by the English cabinet, and in Parliament, even his authority was questioned. Whatever differences of opinion might have existed on that point, there can be no question that what he did was eminently well done. The undoing of it would eventually cost the lives of several thousand English troops in the subsequent expedition under Sir Ralph Abercromby; and this is to say nothing of the immense expense that was incurred by the British government to conduct that invasion. The result was that the French army was returned to France under almost the precise conditions as those of the repudiated Convention of El Arisch; but Sir Sidney had done it without the sacrifice of either blood or treasure, and with glory to England and honor to himself

Sir Walter Scott states, however:

When the British government received advice of this convention, they refused to ratify it on the ground that Sir Sidney Smith had exceeded his powers in entering into it. The Earl of Elgin having been sent out as plenipotentiary to the Porte, it was asserted that Sir Sidney's ministerial powers were superseded by his appointment.

Such was the alleged informality on which the treaty fell to the ground; but the truth was, that the

arrival of Kléber and his army in the sou[...]
at the very moment when the successes [...]
gave strong hopes of making some impre[...]
frontier, might have had a most material
the events of the war.

Lord Keith, therefore, who comman[...]
Mediterranean, received orders not to permit the
passage of the French Egyptian army, and the Treaty
of El Arisch was in consequence broken off." [1]

For the moment, all remained quiet after Kléber's death,
while the British government worked with the Sublime
Porte[2] for another campaign to wrest Egypt from the French.
A British army was to land near Alexandria, and act in
concert with another large Turkish army collecting in
Palestine, which would again cross the desert and advance
upon Cairo. A second army of English troops and Sepoys
from India would sail from Bombay and lend its aid by an
attack from the shores of the Red Sea.

In the meanwhile, Sir Sidney returned to the tedious
duties of the blockading squadron off the coast of Egypt. He
had by this time earned a great deal of esteem within the
French army for his honorable actions towards it, and so
could relieve the tedium of the long idle days off Alexandria
on the *Tigre* by extending and receiving visits from his
admiring foes in the garrison of Alexandria. Indeed, a man's
true disposition is often shown best in small matters, as in
the following incident that occurred while he lay before
Alexandria with his blockading squadron.

He had learned that the Turks held in miserable captivity
a young Frenchman, M. Thevenard, whom he knew belonged
to a fine French family at Toulon. He procured his release
and had him landed at Alexandria; yet, realizing the forlorn

---

[1] Scott. p. 329.

[2] *Editor's Note* - The "Sublime Porte" was the name of the Ottoman court.
It got its name from the gate to Topkapi Palace, where the sultan
normally held the greeting ceremony for foreign ambassadors.

dition he might be in, did not stop with that. He sent to
him, under a flag of truce, the following note of invitation:

On Board the *Tigre*, June 15th, 1800.

Mr. Thevenard is requested to come and dine with
Sir Sidney Smith on board the *Tigre*, this day at three
o'clock.

Sir Sidney takes the liberty to send some clothes,
which he supposes a person just escaped from prison
may require. The greatcoat is not of the best; but,
excepting English naval uniforms, it is the only one on
board the *Tigre*, and the same one that Sir Sidney
Smith wore during his journey from the Temple till he
reached the sea. It will have done good service if it
again serves a similar purpose, by restoring another
son to the arms of his aged father dying with chagrin.

His kindness did not end there; he supplied him with
money and all kinds of necessaries, together with letters of
recommendation and a safe-conduct, to enable him to reach
his home in safety and comfort. [1]

Another equally fine instance of his humane treatment of
his foes is also contributed from a French source.

M. Delasalle, a lieutenant of dragoons, serving
under Bonaparte in Syria, published an account of his
capture by the Arabs, of his being brought a prisoner
into Acre, and of his deliverance by Sir Sidney Smith,
which does equal honor to the gratitude of the
narrator and the chivalrous humanity of the former.
After having spent four days in constant expectation
of death from the Arabs, he was brought before
Djezzar Pasha, where Sir Sidney vainly interceded for
his liberty. The hapless lieutenant was committed to
one of the dungeons, where the ferocious Djezzar had
crowded his victims, and he hourly expected his fate;
but he was happily deceived. The unwearied, generous

---

[1] Howard. p. 125.

efforts of his illustrious enemy at length overcame the tyrant's fierceness, and M. Delasalle was released. Sir Sidney at once had him conducted on board his flagship, the *Tigre*, where he was loaded, he tells us, with all the courtesy Richard Coeur de Lion could have shown to a French knight. [1]

---

[1] Barrow. p. 338-339.

CHAPTER NINE
SECOND EGYPTIAN CAMPAIGN: BATTLE OF ALEXANDRIA

In the first days of March 1801, a powerful fleet of British war vessels appeared in Aboukir Bay, escorting about two hundred transports, having on board 19,000 British troops and numerous artillery pieces. They were destined for a landing in Egypt. The fleet anchored on the spot where Lord Nelson had triumphed over the French squadron less than three years before. It's water was scarcely free from the taint of the bodies of the 12,000 Turks drowned there in the tragic Battle of Aboukir, little more than twelve months before.

Yet, this bay, the only practicable landing place on the coast of Egypt, was left almost undefended by the utterly incompetent General Menou, who now commanded the French army. Only about 1,600 men with twelve guns showed up to challenge the British landing. If 8,000 or 10,000 had done so, the attempt would, in all likelihood, have failed. However, the small force actually present made a heroic resistance.

Sir Sidney's fleet admirably executed the British troop landing, under a heavy fire of artillery and musketry. The first division of 5,500 men embarked in one hundred and fifty boats and was rowed by the stoutest sailors in the fleet. Alison thus describes what followed:

> The French allowed them to approach within easy range, and then opened at once so heavy a fire that the water seemed literally to be plowed up with shot, and the foam raised by it resembled a surf rolling over the breakers. Silently the boats approached the tempest, the sailors standing up and rowing with uncommon vigor, the soldiers sitting with their arms in their hands, anxiously awaiting the moment to use them. When they reached the fire, several boats were sunk and the loss among their crowded crews was very severe; but the line pressed forward with such precision, that the prows of almost all the first division struck the sand at the same time. The troops instantly jumped out into the water, and rapidly advancing to the beach, formed before they could be charged by the enemy." [1]

After a furious hour-long combat with severe losses to both sides, the small French force, which had made so stout a resistance, was obliged to retreat. The gallant conduct of the British troops, the splendid spectacle of their landing in scarlet uniforms and Scotch kilts, excited the admiration of even the French. "The debarkation," says General Bertrand, "was admirable; in less than five or six minutes they presented 5,500 men in battle array; it was like a movement on the opera stage; three such [movements] completed the landing of the army." [2]

Some uneasiness was at first experienced by the perceived lack of drinkable water; but Sir Sidney Smith soon relieved their anxiety by telling them that, wherever date-trees grew, water must be near, and such was found to be the case.

---

[1] Alison, A. *The History of Europe* (Vol. 5). Edinburgh: William Blackwood and Sons. p. 577.

[2] Ibid. p. 578.

The Battle of Alexandria soon followed, resulting in Menou's defeat. Sir Sidney, though having no command ashore, nevertheless took part in it, bearing himself with conspicuous courage. At one point, Sir Ralph Abercromby was unhorsed and mortally wounded in a charge of some French dragoons, one of whom he disarmed after an exciting personal encounter. About the same time, Sir Sidney had his blade broken off almost at the hilt and received a severe shoulder contusion from a spent musket ball. When Sir Sidney reached Abercromby's side, Sir Ralph presented him with the sword he had just taken, and Sir Sidney swore he would carry it for the rest of his life and place it on his tomb.[1]

General Menou's measures to meet the landing of the English were so senseless as to suggest treachery, had he been capable of it. After the British army had landed, Menou hastily assembled about 12,000 men to fight the losing Battle of Alexandria on March 21st. It is clear from his own reports that he could have easily had two-thirds of that number, with a strong body of cavalry and sixty guns, drawn up on the shores of Aboukir Bay to meet the English when they landed there on the 8th of March.

The first division of 5,500 English infantry, with only the muskets they carried, was landing on an open beach. If an overwhelming force, aided by cavalry and the converging fire of sixty guns, had instantly attacked them, the British would have been destroyed. The heroism of the British solders would not have mattered, nor would the bravery of the crews of over 150 landing boats. Such a loss would have crippled

---

[1] Another incident quickly followed. "A singular circumstance happened almost immediately afterwards. Major Hall, aide-de-camp to General Cradock, whilst going with orders, had his horse killed. Seeing Sir Sidney, he begged of him permission to remount himself upon the horse of his orderly. As Sir Sidney was turning round to the orderly, he was saved the trouble of giving him directions by a cannon ball sweeping off the man's head. "This," exclaimed Sir Sidney, "is destiny! Major Hall, the horse is yours." (Howard, p. 139)

the invading army. Even had General Abercromby been willing to throw another division of his infantry against such odds, its defeat would almost surely have followed. The loss of that first division would have settled the fate of the expedition; the Battle of Alexandria would never have been fought, and the French would have remained secure in Egypt, ready to resume, whenever reinforced, the career of conquest in Asia.

On the 21st of March, 1801, the French lost the Battle of Alexandria. On the 23rd of March, the Emperor Paul was assassinated at St. Petersburg, and when his life ended so did the plans of the First Consul and the Emperor of Russia for the invasion of British India by a great Franco-Russian army 110,000 strong.

Thus an assassin's dagger in Russia, and the stupidity of General Menou in Egypt, forever ended, within the space of two days, all the Napoleonic dreams of Oriental conquest. From then on, the struggle was limited to the narrower theatre of Europe.

A large force of Turks landed soon afterwards, and aided in blockading Menou in Alexandria to which he had withdrawn his shattered army after the battle of the 21st of March. More English troops also arrived, and an Anglo-Turkish army advanced in the direction of Cairo leaving a sufficient force behind to hold Menou in check.

Sir Sidney Smith was not permitted to take part in any other operations on land, but was sent back aboard his ship by order of the English general in command. General Hutchinson took this strange action in an unworthy compliance to the demand of the Capitan-Pasha. Along with the other Turks, he now bitterly hated Sir Sidney, blaming *him* for the great defeat at Heliopolis. The Turkish pashas loudly asserted that his prompt notice to Kléber of Lord Keith's disavowal of the Convention of El Arisch, had alone brought on that battle, so fatal to them.

So great was the resentment taken by the Turks at the honorable conduct of Sir Sidney, that all military or other intercourse between them ceased—a circumstance that caused neither regret nor embarrassment to Sir Sidney.

He remained, therefore, with his own squadron, taking no further part in affairs on land, and went about the business of blockading the coast of Egypt. By the close of summer, he saw the French army evacuate the country—in English, instead of Turkish, ships. He saw all the other stipulations he had originally secured at El Arisch once more put into place—with one difference. As a penalty for having prolonged its defense, the French army under Menou at Alexandria was only permitted to take ten guns out of a total of perhaps forty field-pieces.

Thus, by undercutting Sir Sidney's original work, and at the cost of thousands of lives, the British gained THIRTY CANNONS! The annals of history may be searched in vain for anything approaching such an absurdity, at so great a cost in blood and treasure. Nevertheless, that was the sum-total of the difference in results, between the Convention of El Arisch and the Convention of Alexandria.

CHAPTER TEN
TO ENGLAND AGAIN

On the 5th day of September 1801, Sir Sidney Smith finally left the East. He bid adieu to his noble ships *Tigre* and *Theseus* and their crews, which had, during nearly three years, rendered such distinguished service at Acre and elsewhere. In so doing, however, he left an imperishable reputation as Bonaparte's first conqueror.

Bourrienne says: "Ten days before Bonaparte's departure for Egypt a prisoner (Sir Sidney Smith) escaped from the Temple who was destined to contribute materially to his reverses. An escape so unimportant in itself afterwards caused the failure of the most gigantic projects and daring conceptions. This escape was pregnant with future events; a false order of the Minister of Police prevented the revolution of the East." [1]

At one point Napoleon, shortly after he became First Consul, conducted an inspection of the Temple prison in which he specifically asked to see the room once occupied by Sir Sidney. He said with some bitterness to his secretary, Bourrienne: "And Sir Sidney Smith! I made them show me

[1] Bourrienne. p. 195

his apartment. If the fools had not let him escape I should have taken St. Jean d'Acre!" [1]

Sir Sidney embarked at Alexandria on board the frigate *Carmen*, having with him Colonel Abercromby, son of the heroic commander-in-chief, Sir Ralph Abercromby, slain at the Battle of Alexandria. His son had been chosen to deliver to the English government the official dispatches, giving the results of the campaign of the British naval and military expedition to Egypt.

Smith's arrival in London was marked by an enthusiastic welcome. However, the British cabinet was very aware of its blunder in having repudiated his Convention of El Arisch, and did not have the courage and magnanimity to confer the honors and promotion justly due him. By withholding that recognition, there would be no embarrassing comparison of his efforts with the course they eventually chose. This, of course, was just fine with those highly placed persons in the naval service whose jealousy and dislike of Sir Sidney has already been mentioned in these pages.

The English people, however, could not be so easily blinded to the truth. The constituency of Rochester elected him to a seat in Parliament, which he faithfully held until the renewal of the war called him again to service afloat.

In command of a squadron, he was actively employed along the French coast in a service whose dangers and difficulties cannot be described here. At the expiration of several years of this service, he was tardily advanced to the rank of Rear-Admiral of the Blue, on November 9th, 1805; but influences too great to be overcome, denied him the honor of participating in the greatest of England's naval triumphs—the Battle of Trafalgar. At that battle, on October 21st 1805, Lord Nelson almost annihilated the immense fleets of France and Spain, and thereby ended any serious naval enterprises by the enemy during the remainder of the war.

---

[1] Ibid. p. 331

CHAPTER ELEVEN
PROTECTOR OF SICILY AND
THE EXILED COURT OF NAPLES

In 1806, soon after the Battle of Austerlitz had prostrated Austria and Russia, the Emperor Napoleon made his eldest brother, Joseph Bonaparte, King of Naples. He sent him to enter his new Kingdom with an army of French bayonets to prop up his throne. The Bourbon King Ferdinand and his court, accompanied by Queen Caroline, fled to the neighboring Island of Sicily, and made Palermo, a city second only to Naples in size, his capital.

The British government at once dispatched a naval force, consisting of five ships-of-the-line, several frigates, gunboats, and transports to guard the island in general, and the straits between Sicily and the mainland in particular, from any attempted invasion by the French. They entrusted the command of this fleet to Rear-Admiral Sir Sidney Smith. A force of English troops was also sent to assist in the defense.

The Admiral found the exiled court established in the fine old royal palace at Palermo, surrounded by beautiful gardens filled with flowers and orange trees, commanding a fine view of the superb Bay of Palermo and the sea beyond. Despite this beauty, they existed in a state of constant dread, bordering on terror, lest the French suddenly appear in their midst. Nevertheless, nearly all the richest and noblest families of Naples established themselves there, and formed a society that was equal in gayety and social enjoyments to almost any capital in Europe.

It is doubtful whether there arose a stranger and more romantic situation than the transformation that occurred when Sir Sidney arrived at Palermo. Upon his sudden appearance with his fine fleet in fighting trim, terror was banished, and a feeling of hope, joy, and safety instantly took its place.

As the champion and defender of a defenseless fugitive court, he instantly became *persona gratissima* there. The broken old King, and the strong-minded but dissolute Queen, welcomed him with the utmost joy. They sought in every possible way to win his sympathy and friendship—a sentiment not difficult to evoke in a nature as generous and chivalric as his. Thus, we find a strong bond soon uniting the English admiral and the Sicilian court.

To the ardent imaginations of the throng of noble and beautiful young women of the court, this strange, handsome, English soldier and man of the world—so different from all the other men they had ever known—became idealized. He was at once the hero, friend, and admirer of them all. He might indeed have been a "lion among the ladies"; but he was also a "lion in battle," as he soon proved.

As his battleship *Pompée* bore away to sea, his friends would wave farewells and utter prayers for his safety from the windows of the ancient palace and from the garden terraces. They knew that he was setting forth to engage in mortal combat with the hostile batteries on the mainland; and with joy, they welcomed his triumphant returns. On one of these expeditions he actually landed upon and captured the Isle of Capri, in the very mouth of the Bay of Naples, and held it for some time against all efforts to retake it.

Othello never had in Desdemona a more sympathetic

listener to his tales of adventure than he had in the Palermo court. However, it should be said, that on such occasions he would always include the gallant deeds of others, and never forgot those of the French, whose courage he genuinely admired, and had experienced a hundred times over.

The court at Naples had long been distinguished for its licentiousness. The Queen made no secret of her relations with her paramour and prime minister Baron Sir John Acton. The scenes of the old days at Naples, with Nelson and his beautiful mistress, Lady Hamilton, were easily repeated at Palermo. The only difference was that Lord Acton was far handsomer and more agreeable than the one-eyed, one-armed Nelson, infatuated as he was by the charms of one vulgar woman to the exclusion of all others.

It is quite possible that there was a "strong friendship" between our Admiral and the Queen. Her age (54) might have been a barrier to our hero (age 42), though, assuredly, nothing else would likely have stood in the way.

However, no distractions, even such as the court at Palermo could offer, could prevent Sir Sidney from giving full attention to his many duties. His vigilance never relaxed—landing arms, exciting insurrections in every quarter on the mainland, and attacking, when least expected, every exposed point. He became a terror to King Joseph and his supporters.

Yet, during the festivities surrounding Joseph's coronation as the King of the Two Sicilies, he courteously and humanely refrained from interrupting the ceremonies, illuminations, torchlight processions, and festivities with gunfire from his fleet. He might easily have done so. Indeed, many urged him to bombard the city and put an end to the celebration of the event. But he said, "considered that the unfortunate inhabitants had evil enough on them, and that the restoration of the capital to its lawful sovereign and fugitive inhabitants would be no gratification, if it should be found a heap of ashes, ruins and bones..." [1]

While Sir Sidney Smith was thus usefully employed abroad, an investigation was proceeding in England that questioned the honor of Princess Caroline of Wales, and several other persons of exalted position. Among those who were prominently, and, indeed, chiefly named, was Rear-Admiral Sir Sidney Smith.

Upon his return from Egypt in the autumn of 1801, his renown was at its height. He remained several years in London, and was eagerly sought in the highest society. His own high position as a naval officer and his great personal attractiveness, which appealed so strongly to women, had brought him within the circle of the Princess of Wales.

Much difficulty is noticeable in the best of the biographies of Sir Sidney in dealing with this scandalous affair. It was, at last, stated as a sort of conclusion that:

> His conduct, at that period, will ever be involved in an impenetrable darkness—a darkness made the more deep and inscrutable by the solemn and yet ridiculous attempts of commissioners and privy counselors to dispel it. We have carefully perused all the depositions affecting the continence of that unfortunate Princess, during her residence at Blackheath, and the only safe conclusion at which we can arrive is, that the laxity of morals, and the licentiousness of the manners of almost all concerned in that investigation, make us feel shame for the conduct, with but few exceptions, for all the parties concerned.

> Whether the attractions of Sir Sidney Smith were only incitements to, or actually the cause of, criminality with the Princess, he now only knows. That he was much in her society and that his attentions pleased this unfortunate woman cannot be doubted. It is no less certain that he was discovered in

---

[1] Howard. p. 159.

her company at times, and in situations, that neither
befitted her rank nor his position as a future subject to
the heir apparent.

This intercourse, of whatever nature it might have
been, continued with unabated strictness for several
months. [1]

Having thus made himself conveniently proximate
to the Princess, [in a place of residence with mutual
friends near Blackheath, who seemed to know what
was going on] he was seen for weeks daily in her
society; and being thus unguarded in his conduct, he
gave too much scope for the voice of scandal to breath
guilt upon the fame of a person already too much
open to suspicion... [2]

We shall, therefore, not go into details of the
evidence which imputed criminality to our officer, but
merely state that first a coldness, and then a quarrel,
having occurred between him and the object of his
attentions, he shortly after forsook her society
altogether... [3]

A curious light is thrown on the proceedings of this
investigation, as well as the argumentative character of the
defense offered by the Princess, in a lengthy letter addressed
to the King, her father-in-law. Referring to a former
deposition by one of her attendants (a witness against her)
which was carefully analyzed, the Princess observes that:

...he says that he found us in so *familiar* a posture as
to alarm him very much, which he expressed by a
start back and a look at the gentleman.

In that dated on the 23rd of February, however,
(being asked, I suppose, as to that which he had dared
to assert, of the familiar posture which had alarmed

---

[1] Howard. p. 177-178.
[2] Howard. p. 178.
[3] Ibid.

him so much) he says: 'There was *nothing particular* in our dress, *position* of legs or arms that was extraordinary...'[1]

And now he does recollect it, we appeared, he says, 'a little confused' A little confused! The Princess of Wales detected in a situation such as to shock and alarm her servant, and so conscious of the impropriety of the situation as to exhibit symptoms of confusion: *would not her confusion have been extreme!*[2]

A suggestive deduction that the kind-hearted old King was considerate enough not to discuss in his reply.

The after-life of this Princess showed only too plainly her weaknesses. Besides Sir Sidney Smith, a Mr. Lawrence and several other highly placed persons were also deeply involved by the evidence taken in this scandalous affair. While it caused a great sensation in Great Britain and on the Continent, in truth, scarcely a royal family in Europe could have pointed a moral finger at Great Britain.

The entanglements already described by no means covers all the royal and noble ladies with whom our gallant *preux chevalier* became involved. However, in judging his conduct it might be well to observe, once and for all, that Sir Sidney was hardly an agent who compromised the innocence of any of them. On the contrary, every one of them was quite destitute of moral character, or of scruples of any sort, and only too ready to engage in such intrigues, whenever their inclinations, or their interests, prompted them. To be fair, it should also be pointed out that such were the social conditions of that time, that such connections were treated with the utmost leniency, almost as matters of course. Indeed, these royal frailties tended to be regarded as patterns for similar conduct in countless imitators.

However, in the military, neither the best nor the worst of

---

[1] Howard. p. 183.

[2] Howard. p. 184.

situations can long endure. Thus, it came about that Sir Sidney was suddenly ordered to leave Sicily to take part in the celebrated attack by the English fleet on Constantinople early in 1807.

He departed from Palermo, after a sumptuous banquet had been given him, leaving regrets behind that may not be described, and bearing with him the following touching letter of farewell from Queen Caroline:

My very worthy and dear Admiral,

I cannot find sufficient expressions to convey the painful feeling which your departure (so very unforeseen) has caused, both to me and among my whole family. I can only tell you that you are accompanied by our most sincere good wishes, and, more particularly on my part, by gratitude that will only cease with my life, for all that you have done for us; and for what you would still have done for us, if everything had not thwarted you, and cramped your zeal and enterprise.

May you be as happy as my heart prays for you! And may you continue, by fresh laurels, to augment your own glory and the number of the envious. I still cherish the hope of seeing you again in better times, and of giving you proof of those sentiments which, at the present moment, I cannot express; but you will find, in all times and places, (whatever may be the fate reserved for us,) our hearts gratefully attached to you, even unto the grave.

Pray make my sincere compliments to the Captain [Dacre] and to all the officers of *Le Pompée*, as well as my good wishes for their happiness. Assure them of the pain with which I witness their departure.

I am, most truly, for life,

Your very sincere and devoted friend,

Maria Carolina[1]

---

[1] Howard. p. 168.

CHAPTER TWELVE
THE EXPEDITION TO
CONSTANTINOPLE

The great diplomatic duel at Constantinople in the winter of 1806-7, between Great Britain and Russia on one side, and France on the other, had ended in a complete triumph for the French. They succeeded in inducing the Sublime Porte to dismiss both the British and Russian ambassadors, and to follow up those dismissals by declarations of war against those two countries. But, unwilling to accept defeat without a last effort, the British government decided to accomplish by force that which it had failed to do by diplomacy.

Accordingly, a fleet of eight ships of the line, two frigates and several bomb vessels, under Vice-Admiral Sir John Duckworth, was ordered to concentrate off the Isle of Tenedos. They had instructions to force the passage of the Dardanelles, anchor before the City of Constantinople, and compel the Sublime Porte to return to peace and a renewal of the former alliance with Great Britain and Russia. At the same time, they were to declare war upon France, or, if these conditions were rejected, suffer the alternative of having their capital bombarded and reduced to ashes.

Sir Sidney Smith was ordered to take the command of the bomb vessels of this fleet. Though so insignificant a post was quite unworthy of his skills and experience, he hastened to join Admiral Duckworth's fleet, which he found lying near the mouth of the Dardanelles, waiting for a favorable wind.

This fleet was inadequate to so great and hazardous an undertaking. To make matters worse, it had the misfortune to lose by fire the *Ajax* of 74 guns the very day before it was to set out. This reduced the squadron even further, to seven ships of the line; but the British admiral was resolved, nevertheless, to force the passage. Aided by a strong south wind, they entered the Straits on the morning of February 19th, 1807.

The Turkish forts and castles defending it were so poorly manned and so completely taken by surprise that no difficulty, and hardly any loss, was experienced from the fire of their great guns in the passage.

Admiral Duckworth then attacked and burned the 64-gun vessel of the Capitan-Pasha, which was lying in the Strait, while Sir Sidney with his bomb vessels captured and burned five Turkish frigates, one of which made a desperate defense. Finding himself confronted by a heavy battery of thirty guns, Sir Sidney landed at the head of a body of seamen and marines, charged and captured it, spiked the guns, and hastened to rejoin the fleet to appear before Constantinople on the morning of the 21st of February.

So far the the undertaking had been brilliant, and the magnificent spectacle presented by the ancient capital of the Eastern Empire thrilled the hearts of the sailors with the pride and joy which only victory can inspire. Knowing, also, that the defenses of the city were quite unarmed, no one doubted for a moment the complete success of this most audacious enterprise.

The British ambassador, Mr. Arbuthnot, was on board the flagship with Sir John Duckworth to direct the negotiations and was thoroughly conversant with the diplomatic situation at Constantinople. Unfortunately, he chanced, at this critical juncture, to be so severely prostrated by illness that the conduct of the negotiations had to be left entirely in the hands of the brave, but thick-headed, Admiral Duckworth. The admiral fell into the grievous error of thinking he was as good a diplomat as he was a fighter. The bluff old seaman immediately delivered an ultimatum to the Sultan, and gave notice of the time he would allow for its acceptance or rejection.

So far, so good; but, from that hour the ruin of the expedition began. In a series of diplomatic subterfuges, which were inspired by the able French ambassador, M. Sebastiani, the Ottomans gained time to arm the defenses of the capital. This was the first of many snares into which the unsuspecting Duckworth would fall. [1]

The Turks with the help of 200,000 men, working under the scientific direction of French artillery and engineering officers (sent by Napoleon to direct the work of fortifying the Straits against the Russians) mounted over one thousand pieces of artillery in the short space of a week. They then dropped further diplomatic pretense, and openly defied the British fleet, whose opportunity for decisive action had by now completely vanished.

Admiral Duckworth, seeing himself thus outwitted, realized that the perils to his fleet at the city's defenses and at the Dardanelles were increasing with every hour. He had no choice but to retreat in the utmost haste with the first wind that would enable him to reach the Dardanelles. Unfortunately, no such wind blew for several days, and when he did succeed in reaching the strait, found the Turks there better prepared for his retreat than they had been for his advance.

---

[1] *Author's Note* - Parts of this correspondence and other details of these rather singular negotiations, which will be found interesting as well as somewhat amusing, are given in another paper of these volumes entitled *Great Britain and Russia against France at Constantinople in 1807* (Parsons – Vol. 2. pp. 131-154.). As Sir Sidney Smith had no voice in this feature of the expedition, those details do not properly belong here.

The fleet again forced the passage after a heavy bombardment on both sides, and effected its escape into the Mediterranean. In the process, however, they lost several hundred men, and had two of their largest ships of the line nearly destroyed, besides the great damage that was done to nearly all the other vessels.

Thereafter, Admiral Duckworth took possession of the Isle of Tenedos, and contented himself with a strict blockade of the Dardanelles. He could not venture into the straits again, as the French engineers had rendered any further attempts to pass them very dangerous and, in fact, hopeless.

After the failure of the Duckworth expedition, the services of Sir Sidney Smith in mere blockade duty were no longer required in this quarter of the world. The following October he was assigned to the command of the fleet off the coast of Portugal—a service which was to lead to events quite as strange and romantic as those in Sicily, but on the other side of the globe, at Rio de Janiero, Brazil.

CHAPTER THIRTEEN
THE FLIGHT OF THE HOUSE
OF BRAGANZA

Without going into the intricacies of the political relations of Great Britain and France with the two Peninsula powers, it will, perhaps, suffice to state that at this period, 1807-1808, Spain was the ally of France, and Portugal of Great Britain. The French emperor therefore determined that Portugal should be compelled to renounce the British alliance, accept a French alliance instead, and close its ports to British commerce. At the same time it was to confiscate all British goods found in that country.

Portugal was then under regency, and the Prince Regent was informed that upon such terms, the House of Braganza might retain its throne; otherwise, it would cease to reign. General Junot was dispatched with an army of 25,000 young French conscripts, aided by a large Spanish force, some 40,000 strong, to carry this policy into execution.

The British government was not prepared, at the time, to land an army to dispute the possession of Portugal with the French and Spanish invaders. However, it promptly dispatched a strong fleet, under Sir Sidney Smith, with orders to cruise off the coast of that country and blockade any port that accepted a French alliance.

The rickety little kingdom, placed thus literally "between the devil and the deep blue sea," appealed for mercy from both, and unable to resist either, sought to evade doing anything at all by making all sorts of illusory promises. In the midst of these feeble efforts, it was suddenly convulsed with terror by the intelligence that Junot's army had crossed the frontier from Spain. It would soon occupy Lisbon, dethrone the Braganzas and divide the country into three parts. The northern and southern parts would fall to Spain; and the central provinces, along with Lisbon, to France.

Opinions and counsel were, as usual in such cases, violently divided. Some advised submission and alliance with France, since it appeared irresistible on land. Others, a courageous resistance and reliance upon the aid of its ancient ally Britain. Others, still, urged the royal family and court to flee on board a Portuguese ship to Rio de Janiero, the capital of Brazil, and a Portuguese possession. There, it was said, they might continue to reign, free from foreign coercion. And last, but not least, to take with them, and thus preserve, the accumulated riches of former ages of greatness, amounting to fully 500,000,000 francs in gold, silver, diamonds and plate, to keep it from falling into French hands.

The Prince Regent came under severe pressure by Sir Sidney Smith, including threats of bombardment of the city and destruction of the Portuguese fleet. He finally agreed to adopt this last course, and frantic efforts were made to prepare the crazy Portuguese fleet, and as many merchant vessels as possible, for the long sea voyage to South America.

Sir Sidney had originally urged the Prince Regent to resist the French invaders, offering to land his seamen and marines to aid the Portuguese garrison of 14,000 men to defend Lisbon; but there was no way the Prince Regent would consent to that course.

Alternately swayed by fear, indolence, and, perhaps, by sheer inability to act, the unhappy Prince Regent delayed embarking, even after he had seen the announcement in the Paris *Moniteur* that "the House of Braganza had ceased to reign." Determined, at all costs, to remove the court and, above all, its vast treasures, beyond the reach of the French, Sir Sidney at last threatened to sink the Portuguese fleet rather than see the French become the possessors of such immense wealth. Thus persuaded, the Prince Regent immediately hastened aboard ship.

The Portuguese fleet was quite unprepared for a voyage across the Atlantic, and still less prepared for caring for the immense throng of gentlemen and ladies of the royal court, including their children and servants, who would take part in this migration to the Western Hemisphere. But, by great exertions, and the active aid of a large force of British seamen sent by Sir Sidney to the arsenal of Lisbon to help, eight sail of the line, three frigates, five sloops and a number of merchant vessels were readied. In all thirty-six sail were now prepared for the embarkation of the court of Braganza.

The scenes of this embarkation are thus graphically depicted by Thiers:

> In terrible weather, amidst pelting rain, the princesses, the queen-mother, with wildly rolling eyes in consequence of her mental malady, almost all the persons composing the court, many of the great families, men, women, children, servants to the number of seven or eight thousand, were seen confusedly embarking in the squadron and in about a score of large vessels employed in the Brazil trade. The furniture of the royal palaces and of the wealthy houses of Lisbon, the funds in the public chests, the money which the Regent had for some time past taken care to amass, that which the fugitive families were able to procure, all lay on the quays of the Tagus, half-buried in the mud, before the eyes of an astounded population, alternately melted by so

grievous a spectacle, and irritated at so cowardly a flight, which left it without government and without means of defense.

Everything was embarked by the 27th of November, and thirty-six ships of war or merchantmen, ranged around the admiral's ship in the middle of the Tagus, as broad before Lisbon as an arm of the sea, waited for a favorable wind, while a population of three hundred thousand souls, divided between grief, anger, curiosity and terror, sorrowfully gazed at them. At the mouth of the Tagus the English fleet was cruising to receive the emigrants, and to protect them, if necessary, with its guns...

The Portuguese fleet, having waited under sail the whole of the 27th and part of the 28th, had at length crossed in the evening the bar of the Tagus, thanks to a change of wind, and fugitive royalty had been greeted with salutes by the English fleet. [1]

The Portuguese men-of-war presented a wretched appearance in contrast with the trim British ships, as they had had only three days to prepare for this voyage. Scaffolds were still hanging from their sides, and, in short, they rather resembled wrecks than vessels of war. In the general confusion of the embarkation, parents were separated from children, husbands from wives, and both remained ignorant of each other's safety till they landed in Rio de Janiero.

A tremendous stir of superstitious emotion and fear was occasioned among the immense throng that gazed after the receding ships as well as upon the ships themselves. As it happened, just as the English fleet fired the royal salute to the Portuguese fleet crossing the bar, the sun went into an eclipse, and all mournfully repeated the words: *"The House of Braganza has ceased to reign!"*

---

[1] Theirs, L. A. (1894). *History of the Consulate and the Empire of France Under Napoleon* (Vol. 5). Philadelphia: J.B. Lippincott Co.

During this strange scene, the first battalions of Junot's grenadiers were hurriedly entering the open, unresisting gates of Lisbon—a bit too late to seize the fleeing court and fleet, laden with its vast treasures.

By another coincidence, which deeply affected the people, Lisbon thus tamely surrendered to its new masters on the eve of the anniversary on which, a hundred and sixty-seven years before, Portugal had thrown off the yoke of Spain, and re-established their national independence.

Truly, the cup of humiliation ran over on that bitter day for the unhappy little kingdom whose people regarded the ominous eclipse of the sun as a sign that heaven itself, as well as its own rulers, had forsaken them.

Rear-Admiral Smith detached four of his ships of the line under Captain Moore to form an escort for this royal *cortège*, with orders to see it safely to Rio de Janiero. This was, doubtless, the strangest and most pathetic crossing ever made of the Atlantic.

This narrow escape of the court of Portugal and its immense treasures was entirely due to the strenuous—even high-handed—measures of Sir Sidney Smith. Yet, it was Lord Strangford, the British minister at Lisbon—who had wholly failed to induce the royal Portuguese family to emigrate to Brazil—who received the honors for the accomplishment. Sir Sidney was, once again, neglected. This was yet another significant proof of the political jealousy and dislike which pursued him in high quarters at home.

It is quite impossible to measure the value or the importance of the service Sir Sidney rendered to England in snatching the Braganza treasure from the outstretched hands of the French emperor. If Napoleon had had that wealth in his possession, and employed it with his consummate ability, it would have been more potent than an army of 100,000 men. Conversely, the loss of that treasure was a greater blow to his power than the loss of any two or three ordinary battles would have been.

CHAPTER FOURTEEN
PROTECTOR OF BRAZIL AND THE EXILED COURT OF LISBON

On the 15th of January 1808, Rear-Admiral Sir Sidney Smith received orders to sail for Brazil with two more ships of the line, and assume command of the entire British fleet of six ships of the line and a number of smaller vessels. From his station at Rio de Janiero, he was ordered to protect that city, as well as Brazil itself, from any raiding squadrons of the French, who were quite capable of sending out a fleet from Brest or Toulon.

Upon his arrival at Rio de Janiero the Admiral found the royal exiles and court already established in considerable splendor and comfort, thanks to an almost unlimited supply of gold and the great quantities of rich furnishings and plate that had been brought over by the fleet from the palaces at Lisbon and Cintra. The harbor of Rio de Janiero is one of the best in the world, and the beauty of the country and scenery around it is hard to equal.

He selected a suitable anchorage for his fleet, well away from all the other shipping in the harbor, in order to preserve the discipline as well as the health of his crews. He then caused his ships to be as fully repaired as the resources of the port allowed—refitted as to rigging, scraped and painted—so that they were all soon in fine condition and ready to put to sea for active service against any hostile fleet. That fleet, however, never appeared and Sir Sidney was left with no more serious employment than cruises along the Brazilian coast. He also caused complete soundings of the harbor and channels to be made, and was thus able to prepare a better chart of those waters than either the Portuguese or the British admiralty could furnish.

The wife of the Prince Regent of Portugal was the Princess Carlotta, daughter to Charles IV, King of Spain, and was possessed of some beauty, considerable intelligence, and ambition enough to engage her for years in intrigues to place herself on the throne of Spain.

About this time, Charles IV and his son Ferdinand VII, who had displaced his father by a revolution at Aranjuez, had both been induced by Napoleon to abdicate their rights to the Spanish throne. They would remain as his pensioners in France, along with the rest of the Spanish royal family. The Princess Carlotta, however, decided to assert her claims not only as the next in the succession to the throne but, also, to the immediate government of Spain as its hereditary Regent. She sought to induce the Spanish tribunals to acknowledge her claims, and sent several missions from Rio de Janiero to Cadiz, to London, and elsewhere in Europe to make her case.

The Council of Castile actually recognized Carlotta's claims, but the Regents of Spain would pay no attention to them. Nevertheless, her agent, Pedro Souza, renewed his intrigues when the Cortes assembled at Cadiz and, by the liberal use of money, obtained from the majority of its members a secret acknowledgment of the claims of the Princess.

Carlotta did not scruple, at the same time, to use all her arts and fascinations to enlist the sympathy and support of Sir Sidney Smith to her cause. Under the influence of her persuasions, he readily fell in with her ambitious views especially since his own government began by favoring them.

Accordingly, he actively assisted her and exerted powerful influence on her behalf in London. Thus, for a while, all went well at Rio, where political intrigues served almost as a means to kill time. Romance, gallantry and, perhaps, even love held high carnival in that distant capital, whose passionate royal princesses set an example of levity in conduct that was eagerly followed by the ardent young noble ladies of the court. Their admiration for Smith, this strange, fascinating Englishman, was as intense as had been that of the fair exiles at far distant Palermo.

Garden parties, the opera, balls and banquets, set upon an elaborate scale of luxury, served to amuse and entertain the indolent throng. Our admiral made a fitting return with a handsome reception for the royal family and court on board his ships. To do this, he caused another ship of the line, equal in size, to be lashed alongside of his flagship, and wide gangways, curtained and carpeted, were laid to connect the two ships. The decks of the one ship were cleared and furnished for the reception and ball, and of the other for the banquet. A multitude of lights, superb decorations of flowers, palms, etc., wines in profusion, and fine music, lent a peculiar charm to this entertainment beneath the stars of the glittering Southern Cross. Under the rays of the full tropic moon, a brilliant throng in court dresses shimmering with diamonds, and English and Portuguese officers whose gorgeous uniforms were covered with decorations, danced, and flirted.

However, news of a sinister change in London now began to chill the hopes that had run so high with Carlotta's intrigues in Spain. At the outset, the British cabinet had favored her claims to be declared hereditary Regent of Spain; but, afterwards, changed its mind. Under the pressure of strong political and military factors, they opted for open opposition to the Princess Carlotta. This unexpected reversal of British policy produced the great confusion and uneasiness in court circles at Rio de Janiero, but which need not be described here other than to state that it finally resulted in the complete defeat of all the ambitious hopes and restless intrigues of Carlotta.

Under this sudden and complete change of policy in London, the strong support openly given by Sir Sidney Smith to the plans of the Princess now invoked the marked displeasure of the British government. Smith's enemies at home did not fail to take advantage. They had him replaced in June 1809, and recalled to England.

Thus were the warm ties suddenly broken that had made life for him as bright in the beautiful capital of the Southern Hemisphere, as it had been in the enchanting days at Palermo. Amid the heartfelt regrets, adieus, and tears of some of the exiled court at Rio de Janiero, he embarked on his flagship for home, where he was warmly welcomed everywhere, despite the jealousy and dislike for him in certain high places.

The withdrawal of France from any further serious naval enterprises left the British navy with little to do, outside of blockade duties on the enemy's coasts. On the 31st of July 1810, Sir Sidney was, at last, promoted to Vice-Admiral; and, in the summer of 1812, he was sent to the Mediterranean as second in command of the British fleets under Admiral Sir Edward Pellew.

Under the incessant efforts of Emperor Napoleon to create a strong new navy for France, they had again attained a rather formidable strength. Smith's job was to bottle up the French fleet at Toulon; but all his vigilance, during the two years that followed, was not rewarded with any opportunity to meet a hostile fleet in battle. The French simply did not venture out upon the open sea.

It was no very great run to cross the Tyrrhenian Sea to Palermo, and he did not fail, as opportunity offered, to revisit and be welcomed by his faithful friends amid those never-to-be-forgotten scenes. Queen Caroline, however, was no longer there, having been obliged to reside in Vienna since the year 1811. Even so, it was not too late to gather up some of the silken strands of a past not wholly forgotten on either side. Sir Sidney was the companion of reigning kings as well as of queens and princesses. But, he also found the time to handsomely entertain the recently exiled King of Sardinia, on board his flagship *Hibernia* in the harbor of Cagliari, where he had come on some diplomatic business.

With the restoration of the Bourbons to the throne of France in 1814, his active career in the British navy ended. Along with many other officers, he received the K. C. B. [Knight Commander, Order of the Bath] in the year 1815. [1] More demonstrations of popular admiration for him followed upon his return to England, and the freedom of the City of Plymouth was voted to him by the mayor and presented in a silver box.

Finally, on July 19, 1821, he was made a full Admiral of the Red in the British navy.

---

[1] *Editor's Note* – It's true that Sir Sidney was finally made a British (as opposed to a Swedish) knight. But, even at that, for all he had done, he was given the second highest rank, in the fourth-most senior of the British orders. It was an award that was usually "bestowed on officers for good but ordinary services." Later on, in 1838, when Sidney Smith was 74 years old, the young Queen Victoria promoted him to Knight Grand Cross. To make even this the highest award given to the person who did so much is, to this writer's thinking, an insult. As I mentioned in the foreword to this book, it is something that, I believe, needs to be posthumously rectified by Queen Elizabeth.

CHAPTER FIFTEEN
COMBATING WHITE SLAVERY
IN THE BARBARY STATES

Sir Sidney Smith's usefulness and activities did not cease when he left the active sea-service in 1814. He lobbied the union of all the orders of knighthood in Europe for the abolition of white slavery by the corsairs of North Africa, the evils of which had excited his indignation and pity, even during his service in the Mediterranean.

He published in London, August 31, 1814, his *"Memorial upon the Necessity and the Means to Exterminate the Pirates of the Barbarian Nations,"* and presented it for consideration at the reunion of all the knights of the European orders, which took place at Vienna, December 29, 1814. [1] In it he said,

> Whilst the means of abolishing the slave-trade of the Negro on the western coast of Africa are discussed, . . . it is astonishing that no attention has been turned to the Northern coasts of this same Continent, which is inhabited by Turkish pirates, who not only oppress the natives in their neighborhood,

---

[1] *Editor's Note*–The full text of this document is reprinted in Appendix A.

but carry them off and dispose of them as slaves, in order to employ them in armed vessels, to tear away from their firesides the honest cultivators of the soil, and the peaceable inhabitants of the shores of Europe.

This shameful piracy is not only revolting to humanity, but it fetters commerce in the most disastrous manner, since, at present, mariners can neither navigate the Mediterranean nor the Atlantic in a merchant vessel, without the fear of being carried off by pirates, and led away into slavery in Africa.

The Algerine government is composed of an orta, or regiment of Janizaries, revolted soldiers assuming not to recognize, even in appearance, the authority of the Ottoman Porte, who, however, does not acknowledge this independence. The Dey is always that individual of the orta who has the most distinguished himself by his cruelty, and in enriching his confederates by permitting them to practice all manner of violence in Africa, and piracies at sea, against the weaker European nations, or those whose immediate vengeance it does not fear... This barbarian has also another formidable method of extorting money from Christian princes: he threatens them, as he has just served Sicily, to put to death all their subjects that may fall into his power; his well-known cruelty rendering these threats the more formidable, because to him the means of making use of the money of one Christian prince to carry on the war that he has declared against another; he can thus place all Europe under contribution, and force, in a manner, nations, each in its turn, to pay tribute to his ferocity, in purchasing from him the lives of the unfortunate slaves, and peace. It is useless to demonstrate that such a state of things is not only monstrous but absurd, and that it no less outrages religion than humanity and honor.

This eloquent and powerful appeal, excited the greatest interest not only at Vienna, but throughout Europe, and we learn that the Memorial was "Received, considered and adopted at Paris, September, 1814; at Turin, October 14, 1814, and at Vienna, during the meeting of the Congress of the Allied Sovereigns."

It is impossible to know what might have developed from this outburst of European indignation, as the sudden return of Napoleon from Elba in February 1815 so convulsed Europe that no further concerted action by the Knights could occur. But Sir Sidney had, nevertheless, provided the impetus that caused the British government to dispatch a naval expedition in 1816, under Lord Exmouth, that bombarded and reduced the defenses of Algiers to a heap of ruins. This, in turn, caused the liberation of every white captive, the payment of damages, and solemn promises by the Dey of a full reform of his outrageous methods.

There was, however, a widespread feeling that the command of this great punitive expedition should have been given to the man who had not merely inspired it, but was, in truth, by far the ablest living naval officer of Great Britain— Vice-Admiral Sir Sidney Smith. It would have afforded a glorious and well-deserved finale to a splendid career. But here, as so often before, the venom of political jealousy and personal pique was to again deprive this heroic man of his earned right to honorable distinction.

CHAPTER SIXTEEN
A PERMANENT RESIDENCE
AT LAST—IN PARIS

It can hardly be supposed that this final act of cold injustice, added to those that had preceded it, would not profoundly affect someone as proud as Sir Sidney Smith. Indeed, it might have had much to do with his choosing Paris for his residence for the rest of his life. We simply don't know, because in his surviving writings Sir Sidney never offered a complaint. [1]

On the other hand, it might be imagined that, as a cosmopolitan man of the world, he had long since learned to accept the disappointments of life in a true spirit of philosophical resignation, not to say indifference. Again, we just don't know. We do know, however, that he had not soured on his country, which remained glorious and beloved for him to the end.

Quite apart from this, however, there were, in truth, many reasons why Paris should, upon the restoration of peace, attract at once throngs of the rich and the educated

---

[1] *Editor's Note* - Unfortunately, much of Sir Sidney's correspondence was placed into storage and later destroyed in a fire.

from all countries. Now that it could, once more, be safely approached, it possessed all the curious power of attraction, which makes everyone wish to behold with his own eyes the places from which such tremendous detonations and upheavals had come.

Indeed, what spot on earth could compare in interest with a city that still sparkled with the glorious days of the Empire? There were still to be found the heroic remnants of those warriors who had raised France to the pinnacle of glory. A thousand absorbing memories permeated the very atmosphere of Paris.

The half-extinguished embers of the Revolution, of the Reign of Terror, seemed even then to linger in its streets. Everywhere there were gloomy fanatics and ferocious Jacobins who were as ready to cry *Vive la Révolution,* as the Royalists were to answer with *Vive le Roi,* or the defiant veterans with *Vive l'Empereur!*

But above all, and beyond all, it was still the Emperor who filled the thoughts and excited the admiration of even his enemies. Though chained to the distant Rock of St. Helena, he could not be banished from the hearts of his people and his army. Europe felt this and, in terror and bitterness, the wretched Bourbons realized that France still belonged, not to them, *but to him!*

The Paris he had done so much to adorn and beautify remained, more than ever, the social and cultural capital of the world. Upon one possessed of the intellectual attainments of Sir Sidney Smith, such a city acted like a powerful magnet. To such a nature as his, endowed as it was with rare social qualities and the highest culture, the heavy dullness of London society had long since become repulsive, cursed as it was with the coarse dissipations and unrestrained drunkenness that characterized it at that time.

In Sir Sidney's youth, and in the absence of any other point of comparison, it had been tolerable enough. But, in truth, London society had become stagnant and had advanced neither in culture nor intellect, while Smith had far outgrown it in both. With peace, the disbanding of most of the military and naval forces, coupled with the severe financial distress that began in 1816, England became intolerably dull. London beheld with envy the rich and idle of every country who hasten to Paris to squander their millions.

Europe looked with indifference upon England, now that the golden stream of guineas had ceased to enrich and tempt it to make war upon Napoleon. London sunk in the intellectual and social scale nearly to the level of such capitals as Vienna and St. Petersburg.

For Sir Sidney "the Fog Babylon," as Carlyle called it, had become impossible as a place of residence, especially when Paris stood ready to welcome him, as it did no other Englishman. Besides, he ardently desired to examine with his own eyes the scenes, and to meet the actors in the most stupendous revolution the human race had ever known. He spoke the French language perfectly, and was well read in its literature.

Furthermore, despite the hard blows given and received by both sides in the war, Sir Sidney Smith understood and admired the French. In return, the French understood and admired Sir Sidney Smith as one of the bravest, and altogether the most honorable of all their late foes. They remembered, for example, his behavior towards the French army in Egypt when he could have betrayed them and caused their surrender. Instead, he nobly adhered to the dictates of honor, and that was most gratefully remembered by the French nation.

Under such conditions, our Admiral, as distinguished in dress, manner, and bearing as the most aristocratic and punctilious of the Gauls themselves, was welcomed in every circle he chose to enter in France. His friendships soon included names illustrious in the military and civil annals of the past twenty-five years, not merely of France, but of all Europe. Paris had become, in a sense, the social as well as the intellectual capital of Europe, where the enlightened of all nations might meet in unrestrained social intercourse.

As to the character and manners of Sir Sidney, it was said of him at the time that:

> His presence is esteemed an honor in every society, and his amiable and entertaining manners are a charm in every company, while his intellectual acquirements are of the highest order... [1]

> His heart, indeed, is the source of all good and elevated actions, and his conduct, on many occasions, recalls that beautiful saying of the moralist: 'I desire to be happy, but I live in society with other men who also desire to be happy; let us then endeavor to discover the means by which I can augment my own happiness, whilst I add to, or, at least, do not diminish, that of others.' [2]

> Sir Sidney was ever actuated by the most liberal and farsighted views. Where there was the great accumulation of misery, there was his gallant and gentle heart. [3]

Honored and esteemed at home as well as abroad, he passed his remaining years in the enjoyment of the most congenial and elevated social surroundings in Paris, which had grown dear to him. He died there on the 26th day of May 1840, and thus ended, amid universal regrets, a life that in extent, variety, and romance of adventure, as well as splendid, heroic achievement, can scarcely be paralleled.

He was interred, after imposing funeral ceremonies, in France's great necropolis, the Cemetery of Père Lachaise, crowded with its 300,000 tenants. There he rests beneath a handsome marble monument facing the *Chemin des Anglais* [Road of the English].

---

[1] Howard. p. 380.

[2] Ibid.

[3] Ibid.

He lies at no great distance from those of a host of illustrious heroes and lieutenants of Napoleon Bonaparte, the Great Captain, whose sepulcher rises in solitary grandeur just across the Seine. Ney, "the Bravest of the Brave," Murat, the Magnificent, the Master-General of the Cavalry of the Empire, Massena, Davout, Suchet, Oudinot—marshals and warriors whose names will be remembered with admiration when all the paltry, princely titles of nobility are forgotten.

They are assembled here, almost within the sound of Bonaparte's voice, awaiting the Great Final Muster upon the summits of those lofty, shaded heights. They no longer need the ceaseless roar of Paris, whose restless, seething, tide of life was once so familiar to them all; yet that tide, like that of the sea, ever sweeps around the massive gray walls which mark the confines between the living and the dead.

TOULON—ACRE—EL ARISCH—LISBON—are glorious names in Sir Sidney Smith's career, which, in their tremendous consequences, rendered him a decisive actor in the mighty Napoleonic drama. They truly entitle him to be classed with Wellington and Nelson in the galaxy of great British heroes.

APPENDIX A
Memorial Upon the Necessity and the Means to Exterminate the Pirates of the Barbarian Nations
London, August 31, 1814

Whilst the means of abolishing the slave-trade of the negro on the western coast of Africa are discussed, and whilst civilised Europe is endeavouring to extend the benefits of commerce, and of the security of person and property into the interior of this vast continent, peopled with a race of men naturally mild and industrious, and capable of enjoying the highest degree of civilisation, it is astonishing that no attention has been turned to the southern coast of this same country, which is inhabited by Turkish pirates, who not only oppress the natives in their neighbourhood, but carry them off, and purchase them as slaves, in order to employ them in armed vessels, to tear away from their firesides the honest cultivators of the soil, and the peaceable inhabitants of the shores of Europe. This shameful piracy is not only revolting to humanity, but it fetters commerce in the most disastrous manner, since, at present, mariners can neither navigate the Mediterranean nor the Atlantic in a merchant-vessel, without the fear of being carried off by pirates, and led away into slavery in Africa. The Algerine government is composed of an orta, or a regiment of Janissaries, revolted soldiers, assuming not to recognise, even in appearance, the authority of the Ottoman Porte, who, however, does not acknowledge their independence. The Dey is always that individual of the orta who has the most distinguished himself by his cruelty. He is now at the head of the regency or divan, enriching his confederates, that is to say, permitting them to practise all manner of violence in Africa, and piracies at sea, against the weaker European nations, or those whose immediate vengeance it does not fear.

Even the Ottoman flag itself is no protection for its Greek subjects, in sheltering them from the Algerine corsairs. Lately, the Dey, either through the caprice of cruelty, or by a barbarous policy, the end of which is to destroy the rival commerce of Tunis and Tripoli, has hung the crews of some ships that have fallen into his power, from the Archipelago and Egypt, and which were laden with corn.

The Pacha of Egypt, in his just anger, has caused all Algerines found in his territories to be imprisoned, and demands in vain the restitution of the cargoes so unjustly seized by the Dey of Algiers.

The Sublime Porte sees with indignation, and even with umbrage, that a revolted vassal dares to perform the most outrageous and the most atrocious acts against his peaceful subjects, and that it cripples a commerce, of which he was never more in need, in order to be enabled to pay the troops of the pachas employed upon the eastern frontier of the Ottoman empire, in order to oppose the Wachabites, and the other numerous Arabian tribes, which, under sectarian influence, cease not, by their invasions, to threaten the existence of his tottering government.

On the other side, Europe is interested in the support of the Ottoman government, as an acknowledged authority, and as a power which is able to restrain the pachas and the revolted beys, and preventing them from following the example of Algiers, in becoming sea-robbers. This interests Europe the more particularly, in the need that is often experienced for the import of corn from the Black Sea and from the Nile, countries where there is always a superabundance; whilst, in the Ottoman empire, the bad season of the north is always counterbalanced by the good season of the south in the same year, and *vice versâ*.

Thus, if a barbarian, calling himself an independent sovereign, though not acknowledged as such by the Turkish sultan, his rightful sovereign, may, as he thinks fit, threaten, coerce, and hang the Greeks, imprison the mariners of the small European states, who alone carry on a trade that the ships of the greater powers do not find sufficiently advantageous to follow, because they cannot navigate at so small an outlay; if this bold chief of pirates may, at his own good pleasure, intercept cargoes of corn destined for Europe, civilised nations are, in this respect, dependent upon a chief of robbers, who can, unknown to them, increase their distress, and even famish them in times of scarcity.

This barbarian has also another formidable method of extorting money from Christian princes; he threatens them, as he has just served Sicily, to put to death all their subjects that may fall into his power; his well-known cruelty rendering these threats the more formidable, because to him the means of making use of the money of one Christian prince to carry on the war that he has declared against another; he can thus place all Europe under contribution, and force, in a manner, nations, each in its turn, to pay tribute to his ferocity, in purchasing from him the lives of the unfortunate slaves, and peace.

It is useless to demonstrate that such a state of things is not only monstrous but absurd, and that it no less outrages religion than humanity and honour. The progress of knowledge and civilisation ought, necessarily, to dispel it.

It is evident that the military capabilities employed by Christian princes, up to this moment, to keep in check these barbarous states, have been, not only insufficient, but more often have been operative to consolidate still more this barbarian power. Europe has, for a long period, appeared to rely on the efforts of the Knights of St. John of Jerusalem, and not sufficiently to have understood that this order of chivalry had not, latterly, the power, and perhaps not the energy sufficient to counterbalance and repel the continually recurring aggressions of these numerous pirates. Besides, through the nature of its institution, the order of Malta, forbidden to have any intercourse with infidels, cannot turn to advantage all political resources, in making treaties of alliance with those among them who are rather the victims of this piratical system than pirates themselves; as, for example, Tunis and Morocco, both of them governed by princes born in these states, and who have, for a long time, shown themselves well disposed, and are quite capable of maintaining with European powers social and commercial relations.

Thus, the revival of this order, after the political suicide that it has committed, would not be sufficient to accomplish the object proposed. This object is to secure Europe for ever from the assaults of the African corsairs, and to cause these states, essentially piratical, because barbarous, to establish governments useful to commerce, and in harmony with civilised nations.

Now, what are the means to be employed? The undersigned wishes to make Europe share in his conviction, the result of thirty years of study and of profound examination. He never ceased, during his mission to the Ottoman court, and in his command in the Levant, to occupy himself with the subject on which he is now speaking. It was ever present to him, both in the fields and on the waves of this same power, and during the whole course of those relations, that are publicly enough known, which he had with the nations and the territories of Asia and Africa.

This internal conviction of the possibility of promptly putting an end to this system of brigandage of those barbarian states, cannot better be proved than by the offer that he makes to take upon himself the direction of the enterprise, provided that the necessary means be placed at his disposal.

Animated by the remembrance of his oaths as a knight, and desiring to excite the same ardour in other Christian knights, he proposes to the nations the most interested in the success of this noble enterprise, to engage themselves, by treaty, to furnish each their contingent of a maritime, or, more properly speaking, amphibious force, which, without compromising any flag, and without depending on the wars or the political events of the nations, should constantly guard the shores of the Mediterranean, and take upon itself the important office of watching, pursuing, and capturing all pirates by land and by sea. This power, owned and protected by all Europe, would not only give perfect security to commerce, but would finish by civilising the African coasts, by preventing their inhabitants from continuing their piracy, to the prejudice of productive industry and legitimate commerce.

This protective and imposing force would commence its operations by the vigorous blockade of the barbarian naval forces, wherever they might be found; at the same time that ambassadors from all the sovereigns and states of Christianity ought mutually to support each other, in representing to the Sublime Porte, that she cannot be otherwise than herself responsible for the hostile acts of her subjects, if she continues to permit the African garrisons to recruit in her territories, which are of no utility to her, whilst these forces would be better employed against her enemies than against European and armed powers; and in requiring from her a formal disavowal, and even an authentic interdiction against the wars that these rebel chiefs declare against Europe.

The Ottoman Porte might be induced to grant promotion and rewards to those of the Janissaries, captains of frigates, and others, Algerine mariners, who should obey the Sultan's command, and, by these means, the Dey would soon find himself abandoned, and without adequate means of defence.

The other details will be easily developed when the sovereigns shall have adopted the principle, and when they shall have deigned to grant to the undersigned the confidence and the authority necessary to the success of the enterprise.

Received, considered, and adopted at Paris, September, 1814; at Turin, October 14th, 1814; and at Vienna, during the meeting of the Congress of the allied sovereigns.

WM. SIDNEY SMITH

APPENDIX B
The Sir Sidney Smith Timeline

1764

June 21st: Born in London (Westminster) the middle of three sons. His father was Captain John Spencer Smith, an army officer and minor member of the court. He was distantly related to the Pitt family. His mother was the daughter of Pinkney Wilkinson, a wealthy merchant who promptly disinherited her (and by extension Sidney) as soon as she married John Spencer Smith.

1777

Smith enters the navy as a "captain's servant" and was later promoted to midshipman. His first posting was on the *Tortoise* (32), an armed storeship that had a captain who loved to try to capture merchant vessels with his lumbering ship.

1778

He is transferred to the frigate (Pocock says brig) *Unicorn* (28) where he got his first taste of battle. In a three hour fight the *Unicorn* captured the American frigate *Raleigh* (32). The Unicorn lost 13 men and had numerous wounded, included Sidney who had his forehead opened by a splinter. Smith also distinguished himself by helping to toss the ship's guns overboard when they were caught in a terrible storm.

1779

Smith was transferred to the *Sandwich* (90), which was the flagship of the Channel Squadron and where he served under the famous admiral George Brydges Rodney.

1780

January 16th: He was with Rodney at the Battle of Cape St. Vincent where Rodney cited him for his bravery.

September 25th: Passes examination and appointed lieutenant aboard the *Alcide* (74) despite being only 16 (you needed to be 19) and only having three years of service as a midshipman (he was supposed to have six). Thus, his appointment was not officially confirmed until August 29, 1783.

1781

September 5th: Smith was at the Battle of the Chesapeake (Battle of the Virginia Capes) aboard the *Alcide*.

1782

April 9th - 12th: Smith was at the Battle of the Saintes also aboard the *Alcide*. Rodney was so impressed with his young lieutenant that he gave him command of the sloop *Fury* (16).

1783

May: Rodney promotes him again, this time to the rank of captain and gives him command of the *Alcmene* (32). He thus becomes the captain of a 32-gun frigate with a crew of 300 men at the age of 19.

September 3: The Treaty of Paris is signed, thus ending the American Revolutionary War. At about the same time, and in separate agreements, peace treaties were concluded with France, Spain and the Dutch Republic.

1784

February: Smith returns to England where his crew is payed off and the ship is sold.

1785

Smith lives in France for a while to perfect his language skills and to spy on French seaports. He observes and records the building of the new French naval port at Cherbourg.

1787

He then ventures to Spain and Morocco and again does some freelance spying. He files a report in which he requests command of a force to destroy the Moroccan Navy.

1789

From Morocco he goes to Stockholm to access the possibility of naval employment in their war against Russia.

1790

May 21st: Smith joins the Swedish forces under the command of King Gustavus III.

June 3rd: Russians blockade the Swedes in the Bay of Viborg for a month.

June 13th: Smith is given command of the Swedish light squadron and is the principal naval advisor to the King.

July 9th - 10th: He receives a Swedish knighthood for helping to destroy the Russian fleet at the Battle of Svensksund. At the same time he makes a host of enemies in England because of the many British officers who fought for Russia and were killed in that battle.

1792

May 16th: King George III confirmed Smith's knighthood,

but he was forever after mocked by fellow British officers as "the Swedish knight."

1793

February 1st: France declares war on Britain. Smith is in Turkey with his younger brother, John Spencer Smith, who was appointed to the British embassy in Istanbul. When he hears of the war, Smith personally buys a ship (the xebec *Swallow*) to go find the British fleet.

December 6th: He finds the fleet in Toulon where the British are about to abandon the city.

December 20th: Smith volunteers to burn the captured French fleet and warehouses, and succeeds in destroying ten line of battle ships, two frigates, two corvettes and almost all the warehouses. He would have gotten more if the Spanish (who were supposed to help him) had not been bought off by the French. Even though his efforts resulted in the destruction of more French ships than any fleet action up to that point, Nelson and others blamed Smith for not destroying them all. This was his first major clash with Nelson.

1794

January 15th: Smith arrives in London carrying the dispatches from Toulon. Given a hero's welcome by the people, but no recognition from the government.

July 21st: Given the command of HMS *Diamond* (38), he is assigned to the Western Frigate Squadron under Sir John Borlase Warren. This squadron was filled with skillful and daring captains including Sir Edward Pellew (Horatio Hornblower's patron in the Hornblower series of novels). Smith fits right in with this group.

1795

January 4th: Smith is ordered to confirm the presence of the French fleet in Brest and does so by flying a French flag and sailing directly into the harbor. When several ships get suspicious he, speaking perfect French, calmly goes to the aid of another ship that is in mild trouble. This calls off the suspicious ships and he sails out of the harbor untouched.

July: Smith takes control of the Îles Saint-Marcouf off the coast of Normandy and establishes a fort there by dismembering two of his gun ships (*Badger* and *Sandfly*). This serves as an important support base for the later blockade of Le Havre.

August: At Plymouth Yard Smith designs a gunboat HMS *William*. It featured one of the earliest forms of gun turret in the bow. The 24 pound gun and carriage were mounted onto a bed, which in turn sat on a bearing race made up of cannon balls, thus allowing the gun to rotate in any direction.

1796

March 18th: Smith follows a convoy of nine ships into the port of Herqui. He captured and then burned all nine ships, then captured the forts that protected the harbor and spiked their guns

April 19th: Smith gets trapped when, trying to cut a ship out of the harbor at Le Havre, the wind dies. He is captured, along with John Wesley Wright and Francois de Tromelin, but instead of being exchanged with other prisoners, which is the normal course of events, the French jail him. They are still distressed about his burning their fleet at Toulon so they charge him with arson and with being a spy, and imprison him in the Temple Prison near Paris.

1797

Entire Year: Smith continues to be held in the Temple prison. Although he was not a spy when captured, he became one by running Britain's primary espionage ring, the *Agence de Paris*, from his prison cell.

1798

February 24th: Smith makes one of the most daring prison escapes, not just of that era, but of all time. Essentially, with the help of some co-conspirators, he bluffed his way out of prison with a set of forged transfer orders. He then made his way from Paris to the coast where he was able to get out to a passing British war ship.

May 7th: Smith returns to England and is a hero to the general public.

July 2nd: He is given command of the 80-gun ship of the line, HMS *Tigre* (80).

August 1st: Nelson defeats the French at the Battle of the Nile.

October 21st: Smith is appointed joint minister plenipotentiary (with his brother Spencer Smith) at the court of the Ottoman emperor at Constantinople. This commission was separate and distinct from (and over rode) any orders from the admiralty. This latter fact was not made known to Smith's superiors, which caused the second great clash with Nelson.

1799

March 21st - May 9th: Battle of Acre. Following Nelson's victory at the Battle of the Nile, Napoleon and his Army are trapped in Egypt. He then turns to using his army to conquer the Middle East (Ottoman Empire) and, quite possibly, later India. To do that, he leads his troops up the coast toward Constantinople, but to get there he has to get past the City of Acre. Smith gets to Acre ahead of him and takes over the defense of the city. *In a three-month battle, Sidney Smith, a Naval Officer, defeats Napoleon Bonaparte, on land, handing him his first major military loss ever.* No assistance was ever received from his superiors. Admirals Nelson and Jervis.

Smith receives a vote of thanks from Parliament and a £1000 annuity for this accomplishment. No title. By comparison, Nelson got a Barony after the Battle of the Nile; yet it was Smith's defense of Acre (not Nelson at the Nile) that caused Napoleon to say: "That man (Smith) made me miss my destiny."

October 9: Smith stops Mustapha Bey's army from massacring the Christian population in Cyprus. The Greek archimandrite gives him a cross once owned by Richard the Lionheart (Richard I) while he was Grand Master of the Knights Templar.

1801

January 24th: Smith negotiates a peace treaty with the remaining French forces (the Convention of El-Arish). The treaty is rejected by the British government. Smith is censured by Parliament for concluding an unauthorized treaty and an army is sent to annihilate the French.

March 21st: The Battle of Alexandria is fought, the British win; but thousands die—including the British commander, Sir Ralph Abercromby—and they wind-up settling for a treaty almost exactly like the one Smith had previously negotiated at no cost of lives.

September 5th: Smith leaves the eastern Mediterranean.

1802

May: Smith wins a seat in Parliament from the constituency of Rochester.

January - March: Smith allegedly has a love affair with Caroline of Brunswick, which later becomes a public scandal as, alas, Caroline was married to the Prince of Wales (future King George IV) at the time.

1803

March 12th: Smith given command of the *Antelope* (50) and a squadron consisting of six sloops and two cutters, one named (of all things) the *Lord Nelson*.

1804

April 23rd: Smith is made a Colonel of the Royal Marines.

May 7th: John Wesley Wright, Smith's reputed spy companion, is captured.

September 2nd: Smith conducts sea trials of two new ships he invented (the *Cancer* and the *Gemini*). Based on catamaran hulls, they were designed to easily offload men and cannon onto a beach—essentially they were the first purpose-built amphibious landing craft.

Mid-November: Smith works to perfect a two-pronged method of attacking ships and shore installations by combining Robert Fulton's mines with William Congreve's rockets. A test attack was attempted on Boulogne, but was spoiled by heavy seas and rainy weather. If it had worked, it would have been used on the penned-up French and Spanish fleets at Cadiz, and the Battle of Trafalgar might never have happened.

1805

October 25th: Nelson dies at the Battle of Trafalgar

October 27th: John Wesley Wright is murdered in his cell.

November 9th: Smith promoted to Rear-Admiral of the Blue

1806

January 9th: Nelson is buried in a lavish funeral. Smith does not attend.

January 15th: Smith hoists his flag on the *Pompee* (84) and is given command of a squadron consisting of the

Pompee (84), the *Excellent* (74), the *Intrepid* (64), the *Athenien* (64), two frigates and one Neapolitan. The *Eagle* (74) also joined them later.

May 12th: Without permission from his superiors, Smith relieved the garrison at Gaeta, where 6000 Neapolitan defenders were facing 12000 French troops.

May 15th: Again without permission, Smith attacks the French garrison at Capri and forces them to surrender. He gets in trouble for both actions.

July 4th: Smith proves his tactical theories are correct by launching an amphibious assault on the town of San Pietro di Maida in the Calabria region of Italy, then a part of the Kingdom of Naples. In the resulting Battle of Maida 7000 French troops were routed by 5100 British. Smith's superior, Hugh Elliot, was outraged that he had neither asked his permission nor kept him informed and sent a long letter of protest to the Foreign Secretary. He also refused Smith further financial support, so Smith had to borrow £4,500 on his own credit to continue fighting the French.

September: The King and Queen of the Two Sicilies make Smith a Sicilian Duke and give him an estate. This infuriates Smith's growing list of political enemies even further.

1807

February 12th: Smith sent to join Admiral Sir John Thomas Duckworth in Constantinople to keep the French from forming an alliance with the Turks. Despite Smith's experience with the Turks, Duckworth won't listen to him and the British fleet is forced into a rather undignified retreat under heavy fire.

June: Smith is recalled to England.

November 12th: Smith given command of the *Hibernia* (110) and nine ships of the line.

November 29th: Smith essentially forces the King and Queen of Portugal and their court to flee to Rio de Janeiro,

Brazil, at that time a Portuguese colony. This was done just as French troops were entering Lisbon, and kept the royal treasury of over 500,000,000 francs from falling into French hands. Smith sees the King and Queen safely off and heads to London for further orders.

1808

May 17th: Smith is sent to Rio de Janeiro and becomes involved in a tense political situation. France is planning to establish a base on the River Plate (between Argentina and modern Uruguay). The only way to keep that from happening is for Smith to mediate between the King and Queen, who were feuding over this issue. He succeeds and the French are blocked in Argentina.

1809

May: Smith is relieved of command of the South American station because he, once again, failed to apply for *permission* to defeat the French and returns to London where the public showers him with honors.

1810

July 31st: Smith makes Vice Admiral (the most senior rank achieved by Nelson).

October: Smith marries Caroline Rumbold, the widow of Sir George Rumbold (died 1806), a diplomat and intelligence agent with whom Smith had worked.

1812

July 18th: Smith is given the HMS *Tremendous* (74) as his flagship and is made second in command to Vice Admiral Sir Edward Pellew in the Mediterranean. He gets in trouble again by forwarding his recommendations for the fighting at

Cartagena directly to the British Army headquarters without going through Pellew or any of his superiors.

He transfers his flag to the HMS *Hibernia* (110) and participates in the blockade of Toulon.

1814

Smith "settles down." The war is over (for the time being) and Smith takes up the anti-slavery cause. He creates an anti-slavery organization (the Knights Liberators of the Slaves in Africa) to fight the much lesser known (but very real) white slave trade of the Barbary Pirates. He spends a great deal of his own money, putting him in serious debt.

1815

June 18th: Smith is at the Battle of Waterloo, among other things, arranging evacuation of the wounded. From this experience, he designs a new type of military ambulance. The last French unit to leave the field was commanded by Francois de Tromelin, with whom he was imprisoned in 1796 at the Temple, and who had gone over to Napoleon's side.

December 29th: Smith is made a Knight Commander in the Order of the Bath—the second-highest rank, in the fourth-highest order. He is finally a British Knight; but it is a a distinction usually awarded to officers "for good, but ordinary services."

1817-18

Smith incurred tremendous debts in the service of the crown, which the government is very slow to reimburse. To avoid being thrown in jail as a debtor, he moves his family to France. Eventually the government pays him and increases his pension. He tries to get a sea going position, but he is never to hold command again.

1821

July 19th: Smith makes full Admiral.

1826

May 16: Smith's wife dies.

Smith writes to all sorts of British officials for employment either at sea or as a diplomat.

1832

Smith continues to write to British officials for employment either at sea or as a diplomat

1838

July 4th: Queen Victoria promotes Sidney Smith to Knight Grand Cross of the Order of the Bath. This still keeps him in the fourth-most senior of all the British orders, while lesser men are being elevated to peerages all around him. It would be the highest honor he would ever receive from his government.

1840

May 26th: Sir Sidney dies of a stroke in Paris and is buried at the Pere LaChaise Cemetary.

1999

May 21st: The 1805 Club, a group formed to restore and maintain Nelson-related monuments, restores Smith's tomb. The club learned of its decay from Tom Pocock, one of Smith's biographers.

BIBLIOGRAPHY

Works Cited:

Abbott, J. S. (1855). *The History of Napoleon Bonaparte* (Vol. 1). New York: Harper & Brothers.

Alison, A. *The History of Europe* (Vol. 5). Edinburgh: William Blackwood and Sons.

Alison, A. (1860). *The History of Europe* (Vol. 4). Edinburgh: William Blackwood and Sons.

Barrow, J. (In Press, 2009). *The Life And Correspondence of Admiral Sir William Sidney Smith*. Tucson, AZ: Fireship Press.

Bourrienne, L. A. (1895). *Memoirs of Napoleon Bonaparte* (Vol. 1). New York: Charles Scribner's Sons.

Fitchett, W. H. (1898) *Deeds That Won The Empire*. London: Smith, Elder & Co.

Grundner, T. (2007). *HMS Diamond*. Tucson, AZ: Fireship Press.

Howard, E. (2008). *The Memoirs of Sir Sidney Smith*. Tucson, AZ: Fireship Press.

Parsons, J. H. (1914). *Historical Papers Upon Men and Events of Rare Interest in the Napoleonic Epoch* (Vol. 1 & 2). New York: Saalfield Publishing Co.

Savary, A. J. (1828). *Memoirs of the Duke of Rovigo* (Vol. 1). London: Henry Colburn.

Scott, W. (1855). *Life of Napoleon Bonaparte*. Edinburgh: Adam and Charles Black.

Taine, H. A. (1890). *The Modern Régime*. New York: Henry Holt and Co.

Theirs, L. A. (1894). *History of the Consulate and the Empire of France Under Napoleon* (Vol. 5). Philadelphia: J.B. Lippincott Co.

Suggested Reading:

Barrow, J. (In Press, 2009). *The Life And Correspondence of Admiral Sir William Sidney Smith*. Tucson, AZ: Fireship Press.

Grundner, T. (2007). *The Midshipman Prince*. Tucson, AZ: Fireship Press.

Grundner, T. (2007). *HMS Diamond*. Tucson, AZ: Fireship Press.

Grundner, T. (In Progress, 2009). *The Temple*. Tucson, AZ: Fireship Press.

Howard, E. (2008). *The Memoirs of Sir Sidney Smith*. Tucson, AZ: Fireship Press.

Pocock, T. (1996). *A Thirst for Glory: The Life of Admiral Sir Sidney Smith*. London: Aurum Press.

Russell, E. (1964). *Knight of the Sword: The Life and Letters of Admiral Sir William Sidney Smith*. London: Victor Gollancz, Ltd.

Shankland, P. (1975). *Beware of Heros: Admiral Sir Sidney Smith's War Against Napoleon*. London: W. Kimber.

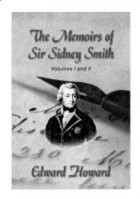

THE MEMOIRS OF SIR SIDNEY SMITH:
Volumes I and II
by Edward Howard

In 1839, Edward Howard, a writing colleague of Frederick Marryat, wrote the first of two seminal biographies that have appeared of Sir Sidney Smith.

In our opinion, Smith was the one man who was perhaps most responsible for Britain's victory in the Napoleonic Wars—and yet is still largely overlooked by history.

This biography was the only one seen and approved by Smith prior to his death. This valuable source document is reprinted here in it's entirety.

The Midshipman Prince is now available
directly through Fireship Press, amazon.com
and via leading bookstores from coast-to-coast

Fireship Press
www.FireshipPress.com

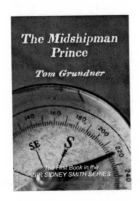

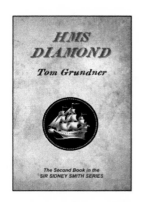

HMS DIAMOND
by Tom Grundner

*The second book in the Sir Sidney Smith
Nautical Adventure Series*

Sidney Smith, now "Sir Sidney," is reunited with his friends,
Lucas Walker and Susan Whitney.

After surviving the horrors of the destruction of Toulon, Sir
Sidney is given a critical assignment. British gold ship-
ments are going missing. Even worse, the ships are literally disappearing in plain sight of their escorts and the vessels around them. The mystery must be solved if Britain is
going to maintain its lines of credit and continue to finance
the war. But to do that Sir Sidney must unravel a web of
intrigue that leads all the way to the Board of Admiralty.

HMS Diamond is now available
directly through Fireship Press, amazon.com
and via leading bookstores from coast-to-coast

Fireship Press
www.FireshipPress.com

Lightning Source UK Ltd.
Milton Keynes UK
13 January 2011

165677UK00001B/61/P